Tarot for Today

Ken Taylor was given his first Tarot pack at 13 years old and remembers feeling a fascinating mixture of awe and delight. Ten years later, by which time he was reading the cards for a widening circle of friends and clients on an almost daily basis, he was invited to set up shop in an authentic Gypsy caravan (all proceeds from this wonderfully atmospheric venue for fortune telling being donated to charity). His first article (dealing with the implications of Crowley's re-arrangement of the Tarot) was published in 1988. Since then he has been engaged in numerous Tarot-related literary activities, including producing *X-Calibre*, a magazine illustrating a previously unpubished card from a different artist on each front cover. Ken has been a freelance journalist since 1992, and author since 1998. In collaboration with Joules, his wife, he has also written a number of books, including *Crystals for Health, Home & Personal Power*; *Celtic Myths and Legends*; and *Scottish Folklore*.

Alternatives
Life Options for Today

Tarot for Today

KEN TAYLOR

LONDON
HOUSE

First published in Great Britain in 2000 by
LONDON HOUSE
114 New Cavendish Street
London W1M 7FD

A catalogue record for this book is available
from the British Library

ISBN 1 902809 31 9

Edited and designed by DAG Publications Ltd, London.
Printed and bound by Biddles Limited,
Guildford, Surrey.

For more information about the author visit:
http://www.wordwrights.clara.net/contents.html

Dedication

To Arthur and Chris Taylor, whose expertise in designing and painting their own pack of Tarot cards inspired me to understand how the cards have evolved through the centuries.

I would also like to thank:
Tony Phillips for his insightful help in plumbing the mysteries of the Golden Dawn and its legacy in the Western Magical Tradition. Any possible misinterpretation is solely my responsibility.
Kai for playing quietly in the study while I worked.
And Joules for giving me the time I needed to collect my thoughts.

Contents

Introduction

Tarot cards are windows into another time and space. Gazing through them we may see the shape of our own future, reveal mysteries of the past, and divine the truth about events happening far beyond the apprehension of our five senses ...

It is this possibility that has always intrigued people and kept the cards in constant use throughout the centuries, but there is much more to the Tarot than simple fortune telling. It is this extra potential that especially endears them to serious students of the esoteric.

Some professional psychics who advertise their card-reading skills for a fee see themselves as continuing the tradition of the gypsy fortune-teller. But there are an increasing number of free sites on the Internet that allow anyone with access to the World Wide Web to have their cards read by a computer. As there are many thousands of Tarot-related sites that Search Engines can help you to locate, you might find it helpful to limit your search by specifying additional keywords such as "free" or the name of the pack in which you are particularly interested. Best of all, however, why not learn to use the cards yourself?

Tarot cards are, incidentally, by far the most popular of all forms of cartomancy, the technical term for divination using cards of whatever sort.

In the following chapters, we will explore the origins of the cards, follow step-by-step instructions to enable you to use the cards for divination for yourself and friends, and discover the techniques employed by advanced students for personal empowerment. First, we ought to familiarise ourselves with some basic ideas.

What are Tarot cards?

Physically, Tarot cards come in a variety of shapes and sizes. Almost all are rectangular in shape, made of thin yet stiff cardboard, and usually designed to fit comfortably in your hand for ease of shuffling.

On one side of each card is a unique picture while on the other is a pattern shared with every other card. The uniform pattern often involves diagonal or lozenge-shaped markings known as *tarotée*. It may be that this is the origin of the word Tarot, an ancient descriptive term used simply to distinguish these cards from ordinary pictures whose back was left blank.

Most Tarot packs contain 78 cards (each of which will be considered individually in later chapters), although a few are rogue. Instructions for using packs with either more or less cards should accompany the pack when bought.

Each pack contains two distinct types of cards. One resembles ordinary packs of playing cards with four suits and is known as the Minor Arcana (a Latin phrase meaning "Lesser Keys"), while the other is called the Major Arcana ("Great Keys"). These two parts contain 56 and 22 cards respectively.

It is notable that the terminology used to describe these two parts of the Tarot pack reflects the tradition that these cards contain secret keys to open the doors of life, love, liberty and enlightenment.

The Major Arcana

Roman numeral	Arabic numeral	Marseilles tradition	Golden Dawn tradition
	0	Le Mat	The Fool
I	1	Le Bateleur	The Magician
II	2	La Papesse	The High Priestess
III	3	L'Impératrice	The Empress
IV	4	L'Empereur	The Emperor
V	5	Le Pape	The High Priest
VI	6	L'Amoureux	The Lovers
VII	7	Le Chariot	The Chariot
VIII	8	La Justice	Strength*
IX	9	L'Hermite	The Hermit

X	10	La Roue de Fortune	The Wheel of Fortune
XI	11	La Force	Justice*
XII	12	Le Pendu	The Hanged Man
XIII	13	Mort	Death
XIV	14	Tempérance	Temperance
XV	15	Le Diable	The Devil
XVI	16	La Maison Dieu	The Tower of Destruction
XVII	17	L'Etoile	The Star
XVIII	18	La Lune	The Moon
XIX	19	Le Soleil	The Sun
XX	20	Le Jugement	Judgement
XXI	21	Le Monde	The World

* The Golden Dawn swapped the position of these two cards.

Please note that to avoid the possibility of confusion (with Minor Arcana cards, for example), I consistently use Roman numerals when referring to the Major Arcana.

The Minor Arcana

Wands	*Swords*	*Cups*	*Disks*
King	King	King	King
Queen	Queen	Queen	Queen
Prince	Prince	Prince	Prince
Princess	Princess	Princess	Princess
10	10	10	10
9	9	9	9
8	8	8	8
7	7	7	7
6	6	6	6
5	5	5	5
4	4	4	4
3	3	3	3
2	2	2	2
Ace	Ace	Ace	Ace

Although playing games with cards for entertainment and gambling has been in common use for centuries, it is only in the last hundred or so years that the Tarot pack achieved widespread acceptance among the general public as an oracle. Indeed, the closing decades of the 20th century witnessed an unprecedented upsurge of interest in Tarot cards both for divination and other magical and mystical practices.

A measure of the Tarot's current popularity is given by the high quality and sheer quantity – literally hundreds – of Tarot packs which are available to anyone who wishes to explore this fascinating world for themselves.

Why choose the Tarot?

There are many methods of self-discovery and forms of divination, but the Tarot is exceptional in that it combines both these objectives in a single simple system.

Another singular aspect of the Tarot's approach is that the cards are their own teachers: all they need is an attentive student to whom they can gradually reveal their mysteries. The purpose of this volume is simply to help speed you through that process of learning, both by pointing out blind alleys and stumbling blocks, and by noting some particularly interesting avenues of research and development.

With regard to fortune telling, although the cards can be used to answer "Yes" or "No" for any specific question, their real strength lies in their ability to solve complex problems with a detailed and comprehensive report. In many respects, tossing a coin is the simplest way to answer "Yes" or "No", and there are numerous other methods of divination that provide us with sophisticated answers. So why choose the Tarot? Let us briefly consider a few of the systems that are popularly regarded as alternatives.

The Chinese occult system of the I Ching (or Yi King as it is also often called) is certainly both ancient and complex. By using three coins instead of the original 49 plant stalks, it is also fairly simple to consult. However, it does have some fundamental drawbacks for the novice. Not least among these are the unfamiliar terminology used to interpret the 64 hexagrams, the lack of a pictorial component to help the student to remember the meanings, and the restricted amount of information that can be derived from any one reading. Furthermore, in my opinion the original tradition suffered a radical and profoundly suspect revision (from which all contemporary Yi King manuals derive) at the hands of "King" Wan in the 12th century BCE.

Reading the Runes, which are symbolic letters painted or engraved on small stones or clay tablets, is similar in many ways to reading the Tarot. They are easily portable and, once their meanings are learned, can be used to answer many questions in considerable detail. However, this Western European system suffers from the same lack of a mnemonic pictorial component as the I Ching. Moreover, it contains between only 16 and 32 Runes, compared with the Tarot's 78 cards, making its scope for subtlety of answer relatively limited.

Astrology is another divinatory system originating in the Middle East that justifiably claims a holistic spiritual element. Its techniques of divination are certainly ancient and may be employed in the examination of subtle and complex matters. However, as its method relies on the ever-changing position of the planets, it is rarely possible conscientiously to answer a detailed question without either several hours' mathematical analysis or the use of a specially programmed computer.

The Tarot is relatively easy to learn because of its pictorial components. It is also simple to use – all you need is somewhere flat to lay some cards down – and very versatile. Tarot readings can also be a lot of fun. Many people use the cards throughout their lives and are always finding new and exciting insights, yet the basic techniques can be learned and put to use by a complete beginner in just an hour or so.

The Tarot is an ancient system of occultism based on natural and metaphysical principles that are as pertinent to the new millennium as to any previous age. Indeed, the modern quest to unravel the secrets of time and space is spearheading a re-evaluation of the Tarot. This reappraisal may even herald a quantum leap in the evolution of our species: the development of a society where extrasensory perception and a heightened level of consciousness are the norm rather than the exception. Investigating and developing our own psychic abilities by using Tarot cards is one way in which we can each participate in this great adventure.

Most of all, the cards have a wealth of wisdom they can share with us at any time of the day or night. This wisdom can help us overcome mental inertia and even physical illness. It can help us to choose the most fulfilling education and career path. It can help us achieve and enhance loving relationships. It can help us to discover and empower ourselves both for the betterment of our own lives and for the world as a whole.

In summary, the Tarot is a powerful tool. And the power to use it lies in us all.

1

Evolving Traditions

The ability to adapt to new circumstances is one of mankind's strongest suits. When it is time to lay our cards on the table, even if the stakes are high we can face defeat, leave the table, and look for a better game to play. You know what they say, "Unlucky at cards, lucky in love".

As a species, we seize the opportunity to learn from our mistakes. We can bend – even break – the rules in order to survive, striving, often against the odds, to do the best we can. The same is true of the Tarot.

Perhaps this is why the reputation of the Tarot today is as great as ever: its value is being constantly strengthened by a popular willingness to explore new methods of use.

Before investigating some of the uniquely modern approaches to working with Tarot cards, it would be sensible to understand how they developed. Only by recognising the forces that created and moulded them can we truly appreciate their structure, purpose and potential.

The cards passed through the hands of some twenty generations before we became heir to them. The minds of each of those innumerable individuals have wrestled with the symbolism and meanings illustrated by the cards. Many have contributed to the store of knowledge passed down to us. Some produced their own variations on the traditional pictures whilst others instituted entirely new designs.

The roots of the Tarot are certainly buried deep in antiquity. Some are so deep that they seem entirely beyond the reach of empirical research. We can, however, trace certain divergent traditions that have branched away from the main stem. It would surely make an interesting interlude to examine and admire some of the exotic ideas that have blossomed over the years.

An apocryphal tale

There is an endearing creation myth which, whilst not necessarily true in itself, artfully conveys the Tarot's spirit of mystery.

All through the Dark Ages the warming light of knowledge was threatened with extinction. Plague decimated entire populations, afflicting equally both fools and the wise ...

Barbarian hordes laid waste the land and mercilessly plundered treasuries of learning as much as the treasure houses of gold. Perhaps most insidiously, the dominant religion sought to preserve its grip on the minds, bodies and souls of the populace by any means possible.

Unlike plague and invasion, the latter force was not indiscriminate, but deliberately and systematically sought out its prey. There was to be only one truth: theirs ... Only one true book: theirs ... Only one way to survive: theirs ... A totalitarian scion of Christian dogma was at war with the world – and the world was losing.

In 1200, a dangerous liaison of libertarian scholars, natural scientists and mystics convened a secret summit in Fez, Morocco, beyond the reach of their persecutors. Faced with the imminent destruction of all ancient scientific learning, these free thinkers struggled to discover how to preserve their wisdom for posterity.

The traditional verbal interaction between teacher and pupil was no longer practical because now, as heretics, they were all under sentence of death. Books were not an option because unless they were the authorised Word of God, they were summarily condemned and burned as the Devil's agents. Anyway, all education – including reading and writing – was monopolised by the Church.

What's left? Well, what about pictures? Pictures of ordinary things, everyday people, commonplace or memorable events: surely they would pass beneath the official censor's notice? Yes, but even if you could somehow summarise the condensed version of the sum of all human knowledge into a set of symbolic images, could they really preserve the seeds of ancient knowledge?

A jumble of pictures certainly could not, but if they were arranged in sequence ... Well, they could tell a story, couldn't they?

Obviously, you have got to disguise the sequence a bit or you would be found out straightaway, but you could build in some clues, a few hints here and there to help people decipher the story. You could even throw in a couple of blind alleys to stave off any lingering suspicion. Then – hey presto: you've got a vital secret formula hidden in an apparently mundane and unimportant set of pictures!

But that was another problem. No one is going to treasure a set of boring, ordinary drawings (especially if they were potentially damning) are they? Even if you could wrap up a kernel of truth in a packaging of pretty pictures, who is going to keep it long enough for it to sprout (let alone bloom and bear fruit) when the devastating winter of the long Dark Ages at last passed away?

It says much of this legendary council, incidentally, that they were confident that a brighter Age would inexorably dawn ...

So how do you make something pricelessly important seem so unimportant that it escapes suppression yet is so interesting that it will never go out of fashion? Make it into a game!

Who else but one of those wise men's serving boys could have answered their perplexing conundrum as simply and with more fundamental humanity as that?

That is exactly what happened: the wisest men in the known world were inspired by a knave to invent playing cards with pictures. These cards have, throughout the ages, proven themselves highly popular for harmless entertainment, excellent for social amusement, and of course (albeit frowned upon) always in demand for that perennial sport of gambling.

Although many people tried to crack the code immortalised by the adepts of the Fez summit and some even claimed success, the final solution remains far from certain, an important point to which we shall return ...

Historical origins

Scholars of history (as opposed to mythology) generally agree that cards were either developed in, or introduced, to Europe through mid-14th century Italy. Indeed, some people have gone so far as to cite the plains of northern Italy as their source, pointing out that the river Po has a tributary called the Taro that rises in the Apennines near Monte Maggiorasca.

In Italy, the Tarot are called *Tarocco* (plural *Tarocchi*). Tarot is their French name. At various times in various countries they have also been called *Taro*, *Taroc*, *Tarok*, and *Taroky*. As we will see, many other attempts were made to pinpoint the roots of the cards by discovering the origin of their name.

Another point of almost universal acknowledgement is that what we know as a Tarot pack is actually an amalgamation of two packs. The Major Arcana and Minor Arcana are believed to have developed independently, being subsequently combined to form the 78-card Tarot pack that is commonplace today.

This theory of separate origins is held to explain the very early widespread use throughout Europe of ordinary playing cards (equivalent to the Minor Arcana), while Tarot packs (which include the Major Arcana) remained confined to a few countries around Italy.

Incidentally, gypsies are rightly accredited with gradually introducing the Tarot to many northern countries, where the cards' striking imagery made them an awesome spectacle in the hands of an experienced fortune-teller. The tradition that gypsies created the Major Arcana is, however, not so easily upheld.

Reproductions of medieval 78-card packs, such as the *Piedmont* from Italy and *Le Grand* [or *Ancien*] *Tarot de Marseilles* from France, are still available, although neither are widely used nowadays. Apart from the superficial matter of artistic style, their basic pictures have remained unchanged over the centuries. Most modern packs still retain many key elements from those ancient images.

The court cards and Major Arcana of those early packs are the only ones to be fully illustrated, the remainder having just pips to show their suit and number. As Tarot historians are keen to point out, the Minor Arcana in those early packs looks distinctly similar to ordinary playing cards. Modern packs are usually fully illustrated throughout.

There are certain differences, of course, the most obvious being that instead of Clubs, Hearts, Spades and Diamonds (the suits represented on ordinary playing cards), the four suits of Tarot cards are depicted with Wands, Cups, Swords and Disks respectively.

In fact, the most substantial difference is that each Tarot suit boasts an additional court card. In the Tarot, the Princess now accompanies the retinue of the playing cards King, Queen, and Knave ("boy", often also simply called "the Jack"). Note also that in the Tarot pack, the Knave is elevated to the rank of Prince. Incidentally, Aleister Crowley's deep distrust of established power led him to rename the King as the Knight, eternally questing for the source of enlightenment, life, love and liberty.

It is curious but revealing that packs of ordinary playing cards carry a wild card, the Joker. This extraneous card, with no suit, rank or number, is precisely commensurate with the Fool of the Major Arcana.

An ancient parallel?

Parallel evolution is a term usually applied to plants and animals which although separated by vast distances, often in both time and space, look similar, behave in almost identical ways, and fit the same niche in their environment. For example, the aerial acrobatics of the swallow as it hunts for flying insects during the day are deftly mirrored by those of the bat that flies at night.

Such natural coincidences are regarded as inevitable in the great scheme of things. There is no doubt that although separated by continents, human drives and developments have often produced similar effects. The famous similarities between Egyptian and South American pyramids is but one of many examples that baffled early students of anthropology.

Having invented paper, the Chinese were well placed to develop the world's first card games, with examples of early cards surviving from the 11th century. It is entirely possible that playing cards were in use during the T'ang dynasty (618–908), when paper money was introduced. Early cards show some resemblance to the currency notes.

The Chinese evolved many games involving cards, including one known as Chinese Chess. This was a game of four colour-coded suits, each with seven cards denoting various military ranks and hardware. There is arguably an analogy between these ranks and our own court cards.

Mah-jong, which can be played with cards as well as with the more familiar tiles, has three suits of nine cards comprising numbers, bamboo sticks and circles. The pictures on the latter suits bear more than a passing resemblance to the Tarot suits of Wands and Disks respectively.

Incidentally, some early cards from Southern China have four suits based entirely around depictions of coins: single coins, strings of coins, thousands of strings, and tens of thousands. Although I have opted to identify a particular suit as Disks, some Tarot packs (ancient and modern) give it the name Coins.

Is it more than simple coincidence that in the middle 11th century the cities of Northern Italy dominated European trade with the Far East? Towards the end of the 13th century, Marco Polo spent fifteen years in the service of the Mongol Empire. It would be surprising if merchants and adventurers took no interest whatsoever in native games of chance.

However, there is as yet no direct evidence to link European playing cards with those that evolved in China. It should also be noted that the Chinese versions are smaller and markedly more rectangular. There still remains at least the tantalising possibility that so far as the development of the Minor Arcana is concerned, the North Italians were influenced by the popular Chinese pastime.

There are also packs of cards from India, such as the Ganjifa, which have twice as many suits, each suit having ten numbered cards plus two court cards. Although these might appear to show suggestive similarities with the Minor Arcana, it should be noted that some people consider the evidence demonstrates the power of selective reporting rather than revealing any actual resemblance.

Another Indian pack, the Dasavatara, contains cards that illustrate the incarnations of the god Vishnu. Could this be more than a chance parallel with the Major Arcana's mystical interpretation as a storybook portraying the progressive evolution of the soul?

Parallel evolution and sheer coincidence are powerful elements of life. We should do well to heed their warning not to take everything at face value.

Tarot as tableaux

The readiness with which many Tarot commentators describe the Major Arcana in terms of a story or step-by-step progression lends credence to the idea that the Tarot originated as a graphic portrayal or as snapshots taken from the story of a mythological cycle, a mystery play or pageant.

We can imagine a carnival procession wending its way through narrow, ancient streets. A prankster or comedian (the Fool) leads the parade, warming up the crowd. Then come the celebrities (Magician and High Priestess) and persons of rank and importance (Empress and Emperor). These are followed with due ceremony by the religious leaders (High Priest) and their primary icon and the cause for the festival – the divine lovers. Whether this happy couple is the Earth Mother and the Sky Father or some other incarnation (such as Ishtar and Tammuz, Isis and Osiris, or Aphrodite and Adonis), they reveal that this is a pagan scene.

Then the military contingent displays its prowess (the war Chariot was once the most formidable piece of military hardware, and used cutting-edge technology). Now we see the lesser agents of law and order, such as the judiciary and the bureaucrats (Justice), and, perhaps, minor or unorthodox religious figures (Hermit).

Next comes the centrepiece of the entire procession (the Wheel of Fortune). We may presume that this device could have represented a holiday, such as the Roman festival of Saturnalia. Here, the underclass are exalted and given all the opulence and honours of the upper class, and the upper classes are debased and have licence to behave in a thoroughly libertine and disreputable manner! Saturnalia was held at the midwinter solstice. There is a notable parallel with traditional Christian iconography here: the presentation – to a mere baby – of gifts fit for a king.

Now the carnival really gets into full swing with the emphasis firmly on entertainment. It may be no surprise therefore that we encounter such bizarrerie as the circus lion-tamer (Strength), the scapegoat (Hanged Man), Death incarnate, and all the other motley crew that go to make up the cast of the mystery play that is enacted as the finale to the procession.

Exactly what the final scenes celebrated seems far from clear, but the *dramatis personae* would be comprised of characters drawn from and representing the various ranks of social standing, the powers of the mind, the forces of nature, and the celestial court. We shall return to the consideration of these players in our examination of the so-called *Tarocchi of Mantegna*, in the chapter dealing with Tarot mysteries.

In ancient Italy, the tableaux that were a popular part of dramatisations, and which were enacted in the streets in the form of triumphal processions (both religious and secular), bore the name Triumphs. It so happens that there is an ancient Italian Tarot card game called Trionfi ("Triumphs") which used only the cards of the Major Arcana. Indeed, it is from this card game that the word "Trumps" derives, a name that exclusively denotes the cards of the Major Arcana.

The game is held as palpable evidence to indicate that these cards originally portrayed a sacred story or mystery play. However, most card games have winners and losers, for it is in the nature of the game that someone triumphs over the opposition. Therefore, we still cannot be sure that this is the true origin of the Major Arcana, only that those cards were used in order to win an exciting game.

Other ideas

Over the centuries, the heated academic debate concerning the precise age and origin of Tarot cards has inevitably fuelled some outlandish theorising.

Some people argue that their ancient, even prehistoric, usage may have been restricted to initiates of profound mysteries who were sworn to silence. Conspiracy theorists delight in considering whether such cabals are still functioning and, more sensationally, what is the nature of their secret purpose.

The imposing ruins and mysterious hieroglyphs of ancient Egypt inspired one influential 18th-century theorist, Antoine Court de Gebelin, to suggest that the origins of the equally mysterious Tarot may lie in the bowels of that lost civilisation. He saw in the cards' arcane symbolism the keys to unlock the bonds of man's spiritual ignorance, and declared that all the occult powers of the ancient adepts could be accessed by virtue of the cards. In particular, he saw the cards as leaves extracted from a primeval book of magic called the Book of Thoth, the ibis-headed god of wisdom and magic.

The *Tarots d'Etteilla* comprises late 18th-century designs based on this supposed origin. It has even been suggested that the word Tarot derives from the very name Thoth. Another theory held that it stems from the ancient Egyptian word ta-rosh, the "royal way".

Such speculation is, however, scorned by historians. Few students of the Tarot regard the Egyptian connection as anything more credible than simply demonstrating the archetypal nature of the cards. The Tarot, it is argued, can relate to many diverse religious systems simply because it is constructed on the universal principles of nature, both human and divine.

The idea that the cards encompass all of life from beginning to end, with its highs and lows, is expressed in another suggestion for the origin of the name Tarot. It has been proposed that the name is actually a cryptic anagram of Rota, "wheel". The importance of the wheel as a symbol arises from observation of the annual recurrence of the seasons and, indeed, of the sun's daily motion. These fundamental cycles are taken as a model for all existence (including the doctrine of reincarnation), and have formed the basis for mythological themes in many different cultures and times.

While we are on the subject, it is interesting to note that this cyclic feature of planetary motion would apply equally well anywhere in the known universe. It is reasonable to suppose that early in their history even extraterrestrial civilisations would have recognised the significance of the orbit of their planet around their star. If and when we make contact, I would not be surprised to discover that they have developed a cycle of myths analogous to those of our own species.

The power of the Rota symbolism could be profound indeed. I am not suggesting that we would find our interstellar cousins using Tarot cards identical to ours: that is one conspiracy theory too far, even for me! However, there remains the potential that such ancient and venerable systems of self-exploration could be useful in building bridges based on cultural exchange and mutual understanding.

23

There is certainly no denying that the Tarot has come a long way in more than six hundred years of public use. How much further it has yet to go is anybody's guess. The main point to remember is that we, the people of our generation, are the bearers of the torch that will illumine the minds of future generations.

We have travelled back to ancient Egypt and gazed far into the future in our search for the meaning of the Tarot. Now our quest invites us to turn our minds towards the realms of angels and demons, and the rigorous path that leads to union with the godhead of the Qabalah.

The Qabalah (also sometimes written as Cabala or Kabbalah) is based on Judaic lore and literally means a "tradition" or "receiving". It was reputedly handed down the generations from first-born son to first-born son. Incidentally, the Jewish *Torah* or "law" is another suggested origin of the word Tarot.

Central to Qabalistic teaching is the image of a tree that links heaven and earth – the Tree of Life. Tales of such trees are told all around the globe. The recurring image is well researched by students of comparative mythology, reminding us of the power of parallel evolution.

Essentially, these trees are maps of the cosmos. Notable among European myths is that of *Yggdrasil*, the World Tree of the Norse – although the folktale of Jack and the Beanstalk might be more widely known – whose crown or canopy shades Valhalla, where the gods dwell. The Norse underworld of *Niflheim* is associated with its roots whilst midway between these extreme realms lies *Midgard*, the world of mortals.

There are also cosmic trees in the ancient civilisations of the Middle East that predate the formation of the Judaic concepts of the two trees of the Genesis story: the Tree of Life and the Tree of the Knowledge of Good and Evil.

The Qabalah enumerates ten *sephiroth* (singular *sephirah*), "numbers" or emanations that link the godhead at the crown of the Tree with the mortal world at the base of its trunk. Here we find an obvious parallel with the Tarot, for there are ten numbered cards in each of the Minor suits. However, for modern Tarot researchers, the paths that link these sephiroth are most significant. There are precisely 22 such paths, the same as there are cards in the Major Arcana.

Heartened by this insight, scholars felt they could now legitimately prove the ancient claim that these cards encompassed all wisdom and knowledge, in the Qabalistic tradition at least.

Each path on the Tree of Life is also directly associated with one of the 22 letters of the Hebrew alphabet. For Jewish mystics this alphabet was, and for many still is, believed to have inherent magical powers. It was the vehicle through which the act of creation was carried out, each letter having a precise spiritual value and magical power that embodied the will of God. As creation progressed, the letters were organised into words and sentences. Eventually, the entire course of history was spelled out exactly as presented in the Jewish holy books.

It was to learn the powers of these 22 letters that medieval magicians busied themselves earnestly, for knowledge is power. This sacred knowledge promised nothing less than knowledge of the future, and even magical control over the entire physical universe ... God willing. And there's the bind, for if you use magic for selfish ends, you are flouting divine ordinance, and there will be the Devil to pay. In fact 22 paths lead to spiritual purity, a journey culminating in uniting with God.

Whether the number 22 is the crucial clue that identifies the origin of the Tarot (the Major Arcana, at least) is debatable. After all, it may simply be parallel evolution once again. The Qabalah is certainly ancient, and its veneration of the number 22 prodigious. Its mystic teachings can have a profound and persistent effect on anyone studying its mysteries. However, the images on the cards lack clear, consistent and conclusive reference to the Judaic tradition.

There is no doubting the conviction with which 19th-century Tarot scholars seized upon the idea. Moreover, their fervent aspiration to perfect themselves in the sight of God and man gave the cards the air of moral respectability that had previously been lacking.

Just as the invention of the printing press put ordinary playing cards within the reach of the general public, financially speaking, so this giant leap for Tarot scholars firmly established the cards as intellectually credible and a significant branch of popular occultism. Indeed, this single idea has formed the bedrock upon which almost all esoteric Tarot study is founded.

The French author Alphonse Constant (who used the pseudonym Eliphas Lévi) is credited with formulating and popularising the correlation between the cards and the Hebrew letters. Although Lévi did not produce a pack himself, in 1889 Dr Encausse – better known by his pseudonym Papus – published *Le Tarot des Bohemians*, which is based on his work, with additional material including Qabalistic numerology.

Just when everything seemed settled and Tarot scholars could really get their analytical teeth into something kosher, a fly appeared in the soup course ...

Variations on a theme

Appropriately enough, this fly takes the form of the Fool – or Joker – of the Major Arcana. In his ground-breaking theory, Eliphas Lévi identified this blithe figure with the twenty-first Hebrew letter, which symbolised pure spirit.

Whilst accepting his basic premise that the Major Arcana reflect the Hebrew letters, a small group of British Freemasons who formed a clandestine magical order of their own, determined an entirely different opinion of the Fool's position.

Not content with simply swapping it for another letter and thereby altering only two cards, they awarded it the position at the head of the alphabet, the very first letter. With one exception (corresponding to the twenty-second letter), every other card of the Major Arcana was necessarily shunted out of place, and their Qabalistic meanings radically altered.

No one knows for certain whether Lévi simply made a mistake, was bound by a vow of secrecy to a higher authority not to divulge the true order (as those British successors claimed), or was correct in his positioning of the Fool. What is historically certain is the overwhelming influence that this new idea had on the development of the Tarot, particularly in Britain and America.

The initiates of the Hermetic Order of the Golden Dawn (for such was the secret society that the Freemasons formed in 1888) taught that the Major Arcana are keys to the paths of the Tree of Life, leading to mystical attainment and the acquisition of magical powers.

Eclectic and rational, their writings and rituals were drenched in ineffable imagery and romance, and their systematic approach to the mysteries was inspired by the same indomitable spirit of enterprise that made Victorian Britain "Great". With strength of purpose and a keen sense of morality, these Christian Qabalists felt they could climb the Tree of Life, pierce the veil of the under-storey of mortal illusions, and discover the divine love in the airy boughs of the illuminated canopy.

In this lofty aspiration, they differed not a jot from the earliest Tarot scholars. Their main contribution was the way they reasoned and explained their detailed understanding of the cards, not merely the Major but also the Minor Arcana. This corpus of knowledge has become the basis for most subsequent Tarot commentaries and recent developments.

The teachings of the Golden Dawn are not only used in the art of divination or Tarot reading, but have become the standard method for the application of the cards for many magical and mystical purposes.

Although the Golden Dawn did not publish any Tarot pack of their own, two main versions of the pack designed by S. L. MacGregor Mathers, and studied by all initiates of this magical order, have been printed.

The oldest, most influential and probably most popular is the pack designed by Arthur Waite, an early member and prominent initiate of the Golden Dawn, published in 1910. This pack is variously known as *The Waite Pack*, the *Pamela Colman Smith Pack*, and the *Rider Pack*: after its designer, artist and publisher, respectively.

The Golden Dawn Tarot was also designed according to esoteric doctrine by initiate Israel Regardie, and is esteemed as the more accurate depiction of the original material that was shared between members of this secret society.

There are, incidentally, modern magical orders that model themselves on the Golden Dawn and use the old rituals. Chic and Sandra Tabatha Cicero, leaders of one such group, have recently produced *The New Golden Dawn Ritual Tarot*.

Importantly, the original Golden Dawn designs replaced the traditional Minor Arcana pips with pictures illustrating their symbolic meanings. This simple innovation made it much easier for a novice to learn to remember their divinatory significance. In these packs, every effort was also made to fill the individual cards with colours

27

and miscellaneous artistic devices carefully designed to portray their subtle meanings and thereby stimulate clairvoyance.

Another initiate of this influential magical order was Aleister Crowley. Following an acrimonious dispute with the Golden Dawn hierarchy, in 1909 he founded a rival magical order – the Argenteum Astrum ("Silver Star") – and went on to publish his own somewhat radical revision of the Golden Dawn material, *The Book of Thoth*, in 1944.

Crowley's understanding of the Tarot is notable for its swapping of the positions of The Emperor and The Star in relation to the Hebrew letters. This decision was ultimately forced by his apocalyptic vision, which declared him to be the prophet of a New Aeon.

Despite his self-proclaimed reputation as an iconoclast, the revolutionary idea of swapping cards to fit ideology was not without precedent. The Golden Dawn modified tradition (swapping Justice with Strength) to make the cards fit more neatly onto their interpretation of the Tree of Life.

Nevertheless, these three initiates' packs and their recent offspring are generally scholarly reconstructions of the Tarot drawn from a modern flowering of eclectic occultism, apparently grown from the same rootstock as the ancient Tarot.

Innumerable modern packs have adopted the idiosyncrasies of the Golden Dawn and Aleister Crowley, believing that these initiates were instrumental in the process of deciphering the enigma of the cards.

The world run wild
Recent technical advances in the printing industry have given publishers the power to produce packs whilst not with abandon, at least with relatively modest financial risk. The resultant profusion of packs has given the consumer a greater choice than ever before.

The closing decades of the twentieth century witnessed a veritable explosion of interest in the cards. Now you can buy fully illustrated packs with a vast range of pictorial themes as diverse, for example, as Arthurian legend, Amerindian shamanism, angels, animé and astrology.

Despite bringing a healthy vigour and delightful exoticism to the Tarot tradition, this profusion of new designs has also brought a problem. Undeniably, most of these packs have been executed by competent artists. Unfortunately, however, it is rare that the world produces an accomplished artist who is also wise with the insight of a sage. It is worth noting that until recently Tarot scholars have recognised their own limitations and commissioned others, governed by precise instructions, of course, to paint the pictures.

Some contemporary Tarot artists not only lack the basic knowledge that has for so long underpinned the development of their chosen subject, but a few even proclaim that their ignorance is really a virtue because their creativity is untrammelled by doctrine.

It is obvious that many modern packs lack the integrity and power of their forebears, but is this really as damning as it appears? I think the question is somewhat unfair. It is like asking whether the experimentation and excesses of adolescence are morally justifiable. The point is that they are a perfectly natural part of growing up; they are absolutely essential to the development of the individual, regardless of how embarrassing some of the particulars might be in retrospect!

If we are to regard the development of Tarot cards in the same light, we can see that this present phase of trying every conceivable permutation is a healthy and ultimately beneficial process.

What is particularly encouraging is that the very attempt to paint the pictures with images drawn from every possible mythology, tradition, and interest asserts the power of the Tarot. It demonstrates yet again that their application is universal and all-encompassing. The next step is to start assimilating the effectiveness, successes and failures of these many attempts to capture the spirit of the Tarot.

But will it be possible for future generations to synthesise the best of these efforts into a single pack? For example, Arthurian myths abound in references to the Minor Arcana icons of swords, lances (Wands), the grail (Cups) and shields (Disks). Amerindian shamanism can take us on voyages into the realms of the Spirit much as the Fool's journey leads us through the wonderland of the Major Arcana. Angels and the infernal hierarchy figure prominently in the imagery of many traditional cards such as Temperance and the Devil.

Astrology is not only used to decipher and illuminate the mysteries of the cards, but relates directly to cards such as the Star, the Moon, the Sun and the World.

Each of these topics is linked to the traditional packs. Each emphasises some element that was already there. By giving it maximum treatment, as it were, modern artists are helping us to explore the full meaning of the traditional pack.

Might I suggest that one day we will find a mail order website offering us a complete set of 78 Tarot packs – each pack devoted to fully exploring one single card of the traditional pack!

Which pack is best for you?

The number and variety of packs currently available present us with a bewildering choice. In fact, one of the most testing problems to confront a newcomer to the Tarot is which pack to choose – and the first-time buyer cannot even read the cards to help make the decision!

Given that few of us have the funds to buy every pack we fancy, it is obviously well worth investing some time and care in making your initial selection.

Unfortunately, although the decision may be far more personal than buying clothes, which you are usually free to put on and see if they suit, few Tarot stockists are willing to open the sealed plastic packaging to let you try them out. Some do have a loose-leaf book that contains two or three samples of the cards from each pack in stock.

Fortunately, pictures of Tarot cards are widely available, both in numerous magazines and, of course, books. Many packs have a book available separately that details their advantages and scope. The Internet, too, has an enormous variety of sites that are either completely dedicated to the Tarot or have pages relating to it. Many of these sites carry illustrations of cards from the packs that are commercially available. Some even sell packs that are not available through normal High Street stockists, or indeed, anywhere else.

Moreover, being such a popular subject, it is not usually too diffi-cult to find someone with a Tarot pack of their own who would be more than happy to show them off.

As a last resort, have a hearty breakfast, check your wallet, and make up your mind with the positive determination to buy one. After all, you may not find the perfect pack, as far as you are concerned, for many years to come, and sometimes anything is better than nothing. Simply hunt down the best one you can find.

Slip into your local stockist and spend as long as you like – or as long as you can stand the discrete attention from the shopkeeper – making up your mind. Study the pictures on the box, and devour and digest the informative blurb on the box. If you find it really difficult to choose between them, do not buy the one you think you should take; purchase the one you cannot leave behind.

Remember that unless you are angling to join or investigate a particular magical order or similar group who have their own "authorised" pack, the choice is purely personal; you do not have to justify your preference to anybody else.

Incidentally, having read so far, I thought you deserved to know that you have already joined the company of Tarot scholars who, for untold centuries, have been investigating – and enjoying – the mysteries of life and magic. Congratulations! Perhaps you've even already got a pack of your own … So, what can we do with it?

2

Divination: in Theory ...

The Tarot has a mystique unique to itself – and every Tarot reader shares in that legacy of cryptic knowledge and occult power. Whether performed in the strangely scented quietude of a gypsy's caravan or in the organised chaos of a student's bedsit, there is something magical in the act of shuffling the cards.

For the beginner, the concentration and manual dexterity required to shuffle the cards thoroughly – without dropping any – may account for the way it stills the mind and excludes extraneous thought. However, in the experienced or intuitive student, different forces are at work. The mind seems to empty itself, allowing the hands to become agents of the cards, deftly ordering them into the one sequence that will best answer the given question.

The identification of exactly what seemingly magical power performs this feat of organising the cards has been the focus of considerable conjecture over the years. Ideas have ranged from the angelic to the diabolic. Some modern researchers say it is nothing to do with supernatural beings at all, but simply a natural ability common to all mankind, no stranger or more mysterious than, for example, our capacity to learn.

However, it is sensible to note at the onset that there is, of course, a contrary point of view, one which is even held by some serious Tarot students (notably those who have failed to find a way scientifically to prove the existence of the phenomenon). This school of thinking denies that there is any such magic whatsoever, declares there is no innate human ability to read the future in the cards, and proclaims that even any apparent correlation between the cards and the given question is purely illusory. It is worth remembering at this point that a true sceptic has an open mind; only a bigot rejects the possibility of being wrong.

Even if you discount the traditional claims for metaphysical communion during Tarot reading, there is something worthwhile that remains. There is no doubt that the intense (albeit brief) relationship that develops between a professional reader and their clients can have the querent baring their soul. Just by concentrating on the art of interpersonal counselling during a Tarot reading, the reader can produce high-quality insights that should be extremely rewarding for the client.

So, even in the worst case scenario, we can see that the Tarot has much to offer … and this is even before we delve into the mysteries and wisdom of the spiritual story that the Major Arcana unfolds.

Extrasensory perception

Commonly known by its abbreviation ESP, this term embraces a wide range of psychic abilities, including telepathy and clairvoyance as well as precognition. The cultivation of these faculties is one of the many benefits that studying the Tarot is traditionally said to bring.

Despite innumerable, successful laboratory experiments carefully constructed to reveal levels of ESP, these powers are not officially recognised by the scientific community as a whole.

However, one important branch of ESP research promoted in the last years of the 20th century produced impressive results. It is based on a standard theory developed by physicists probing the mysteries of quantum mechanics. Investigating ever more minutely the properties of subatomic particles, these physicists encountered a baffling problem. Like fine sand falling from their grasp, the object of their study simply began to evade them.

These tiny particles were not actually acting capriciously. The difficulty was that the tools and instruments employed to investigate these infinitesimal building blocks of matter were interfering with them.

Scientists had been used to being able to choose an object to study, isolate, observe, analyse and define it, and then categorise it in relation to its environment. Now things are different: we have found that the way we look at something actually seems to change its behaviour.

Light is probably the best known example of this. When you use a set of apparatus that examines particles, light behaves like a particle. But if you employ a set that examines waves, it behaves like a wave. Reconciling this apparent contradiction is one of the funda-mental challenges of modern physics.

Why are we digressing into a review of contemporary high-energy particle physics? Well ...

Clairvoyants (especially Spiritualist mediums) have, for hundreds of years, claimed that they need an emotionally conducive environ-ment in which to operate. Indeed, without a supportive atmosphere emanating from sympathetic onlookers, their particular talents often fail to materialise. The presence of a single disbeliever could be enough to doom the entire experiment. It was as if they were trying to light a candle with a soggy match.

Of course, sceptical scientists inevitably concluded that these oh so sensitive psychics could not stand the gaze of cool, rigorous analysis because they were afraid their parlour tricks would be exposed. A reasonable assumption, or so they believed.

Psychics complained that because of the way experiments were conducted, sceptical scientists were bound to receive the results they expected. The experimenters were accused of looking for nega-tive results and, therefore, the tests were psychically sabotaged, albeit subconsciously.

At last, experiments have been conducted directly to address and investigate the psychics' claims of hostile treatment. Results from a number of respectable sources suggest that humanity does indeed have the capacity to sense, without the possibility of using the conventional senses, when a person is observing them. More-over, we can apparently differentiate between a friendly and an unfriendly onlooker.

We are all familiar with this idea and, if we have not had the experience ourselves, have surely heard someone say, "I could feel someone was watching me ..." It is part of our cultural inheritance.

If you think about it, this ability would be extremely useful for any animal, enabling it to evade the clutches of lurking predators. Such a biological adaptation would enhance the chances of survival enormously, soon becoming an essential element of the genetic make-up of the species.

Soon we may have a generation of investigative scientists sympathetic to the basic humanity of their subjects, the psychics, and capable of researching ESP in a rational and holistic manner. It is also notable that we might before long have the techniques (non-intrusive brain scanning, for example) to understand the psycho-neural mechanisms at work. All this could validate the incalculable wealth of anecdotal evidence that our species has treasured throughout history.

The Tarot is one avenue open to all which can help us to learn to recognise and use our own inner powers. It invites everyone to participate in developing faculties that, if realised, would completely revolutionise our culture and radically alter our prospects as a species on the brink of interstellar travel.

Telepathy

Telepathy is probably the best known of these various talents collectively termed ESP. It is generally defined as the ability for one person to know the thoughts and/or feelings of another individual without, of course, using conventional senses. Strictly speaking, the ability to sense the emotional state of others is known as empathy and is far more common than telepathy. It is particularly relevant to Tarot reading because of the possibility that the reader might start picking up signals from the mind of the querent (the person requiring the Tarot reading).

In fact, reading the querent's mind instead of the cards would be a tremendous problem as you could pick up confusing signals and start telling them what they want to hear instead of what the cards actually say.

The development of telepathy is not usually regarded as a handicap, of course, but rather as a very significant milestone on the path of psychic evolution.

It is usually possible to check with your client if you think you might be drifting into their stream of consciousness. Their response to your suggestion – or, more specifically, your reaction to their reaction – that this might be occurring should be enough to alert you to the possibility. Simply by asking, "Am I telling you something you were thinking already?" should give you a clue.

Clairvoyance

Occasionally, a penetrating perception of the client's mind is nothing to do with telepathy. Clairvoyance is a word often used to indicate a truly supernatural faculty, but it also describes a completely natural ability. The psychic ability is akin to seeing a vision.

Tarot readers extend their consciousness beyond the scope of their physical eyes and witness events far away in space and/or time. This may involve some sort of mild trance, but is rare in a Tarot reader as compared to crystal ball gazers, mediums, etc. The techniques for exploring the astral places (detailed in the chapter on Tarot Magic) can be used to nurture this faculty.

The other sort of clairvoyance is achieved simply by increasing one's sensitivity to our conventional five senses.

Our lives are so rich in detail that we spend much of it wearing the mental equivalent of blinkers. How often do we see something, but not really notice it? Your eyes saw everything around you today, yet how much of it can you really remember? Precious little, normally!

Although still controversial, hypnotism has proven apparently useful in helping people to recall otherwise unobserved details, such as the number plate of a hit-and-run car.

Removing these mental blinkers and opening up yourself to the full impact of the moment can be somewhat frightening, but it is certainly worth the effort. It could even be a source of mystical enlightenment. Developing the skill of consciously noticing your environment can be profoundly liberating. It is also considerably easier to practise this form of clairvoyance than to try to develop any truly psychic ability.

Body language, especially eye contact, can readily reveal how a person is feeling. Watching out for shifts in the posture of your client is one way of gauging the importance and relevance of particular topics as they arise in the reading.

There are many subtle ways in which we all expose our true feelings. Tone of voice, for example, or even a telling silence, can speak volumes. Although clairvoyance literally means "clear seeing", it applies equally to hearing and the other physical senses.

Of course, the way we dress, from our footwear to how we wear our hair, also says much about the sort of lives we live. Our jewellery is another open book to the attentive clairvoyant. Obviously, even by itself, a wedding ring can be a dead give-away!

Again, like telepathy, there are pitfalls in its use. The temptation to tell the client exactly what they hope to hear can be powerful, but so long as you stick to the task of interpreting the cards you will not go far astray.

All these clairvoyant observations can be valuable clues in pitching the reading at the right level for the client, but do be careful. There are some clever but unscrupulous Tarot readers who do nothing but interpret these signs. For such people the cards are nothing but a means of distracting the client so they are put off guard. Lulled into a false sense of security, a person is vulnerable ... and the vulnerable are easy prey to confidence tricksters.

In passing, it is worth noting that actors deliberately counterfeit these nuances, with better or worse performances depending upon their ability. Charlatans who use their powers of clairvoyance to cheat the public are themselves susceptible to being duped by competent artistes. The public humiliation and ridicule that such exposure brings does little to advance serious study of the Tarot, but it does clear the decks (pardon the pun) for honest Tarot readers.

Good Tarot readers will use their natural sensitivity to these subtle signals to ensure that the client understands the message the cards have to give.

Very often, people do not like to admit that they don't understand something. Rather than querying the point, they may be happy to let you (and the discomfort) pass by quickly. If the message from the cards is important, you must find a way to communicate the matter. Again, careful attention to these unconscious clues will show you when you are succeeding.

From this technique alone it is easy to see how even when the meanings of all of the cards are learned, there is still much, much more that reading the Tarot can teach us all. Moreover, these interpersonal skills are, of course, invaluable in our everyday lives.

Precognition

In some respects, the truly psychic or supernatural form of clairvoyance overlaps with that other important variety of ESP known as precognition, which is the ability to know events before they happen. This is what standard fortune telling is all about.

In a world full of uncertainty and stress, since the dawn of history, people have sought to find a sense of security in foreknowledge. To be forewarned, so the saying goes, is to have the opportunity to arm yourself against the contingency. Who knows, with a little divine intervention, you could even escape an otherwise certain doom!

This very practical application of the Tarot cards does not require the reader to have prophetic powers because the cards present the picture of the future. However, because of the involvement of the reader in interpreting and clarifying the cards, a reading presents us with an environment that is conducive and well suited to the development of personal precognition.

Unfortunately, the Tarot reader rarely benefits from a detailed account of the accuracy of a reading for a client. Therefore, precognitive ability is best gauged in readings for oneself. Again unfortunately, these personal readings are particularly prone to the subtle effects of self-delusion. It is all too easy to interpret the cards with an undue emphasis based on our own expectations, hopes or fears. Likewise, it may be tempting to claim an accurate reading even where the subsequent events only marginally echo the cards in the reading.

Because the accuracy of Tarot prophecy takes time to substantiate, the novice must act in good faith when exploring this vital function of the traditional reading. Certainly, no claims should be made at the outset for the reliability of precognitive readings. Only with some considerable experience can the evidence for the power of the Tarot be properly assessed.

Furthermore, every Tarot reader must weigh their own successes and failures in the balance of probability. If a client comes to you to get a second opinion on his feelings of impending doom and the cards are not utterly bleak, you might say, "No, don't worry. You are not going to die next week." Statistically, the chances are you would be right, so that reading is not conclusive proof of the Tarot's ability to forecast the future. But had the cards foretold a death at sea, and the person promptly fell off a cruise ship and drowned, that would be interesting, especially if you were researching the power of suggestion!

Learning to be honest with yourself and not trying to pretend to be other than you are is one of the most rewarding challenges that the Tarot poses.

Incidentally, having mentioned statistics, there are some professional Tarot readers who pay scant attention to the cards, relying instead on their own general knowledge, understanding of human nature, and grasp of probability. During an economic boom, for example, it would not be too difficult for a con-man to advise a client that during the forthcoming year, for example, her career prospects are going to rise. He might suggest that her love life would see a period of turbulence (after all, most people's do), and even foretell that she will narrowly escape a serious travelling accident. "Please," he might add for good measure, "accept this complimentary talisman to help keep you safe!" I reckon the client would be back next year for more of the same ...

Please do not think that only women are gullible enough to fall prey to a smooth-talking shark. I think a glamorous femme fatale could reel in most men too, hook, line and sinker, so be on your guard.

Synchronicity

As we have already observed, the power of the cards (and other methods of divination) to reveal events has been the subject of intense speculation.

Evidence for this mysterious power persuaded eminent psychologist C. J. Jung to publish a *Theory of Synchronicity* in 1952. He argued that at any given moment in time, everything is directly connected with everything else regardless of physical distance, and that these connections can produce apparently supernatural manifestations.

Despite its perennial currency as a buzz-word, synchronicity does not so much reveal the ultimate cause or source of divinatory power as describe its effect. Nevertheless, the enduring value of this theory lies in the fact that it has taken the subject out of the realm of the religious, miraculous and esoteric, given it a footing in the everyday world, and made it accessible to empirical researchers.

After all, what seemed on one day to be utterly beyond comprehension and only capable of being described as magical, is often revealed as perfectly natural the next, when the physical laws that govern it are understood and exploited.

In innumerable myths of magic and the supernatural there are instances of human beings performing impossible feats. It is fascinating to consider how many of the pre-industrial fantasies of folklore have actually been achieved by technology. We can fly, explore the seabed, walk unscathed through fire, move mountains, use mechanical limbs, see and talk to people on the other side of the globe ... We have even been to the moon. The eagle of mankind's aspiration has landed, and the future is in our hands.

All of these achievements have been brought about by the use of tools of one sort or another. Adepts of the occult mysteries venerate the Tarot as just such a tool, one that enables us to perform otherwise impossible feats.

Beginner's luck

Like so many of the little mysteries of daily living, such as déjà vu and bizarre coincidences, beginner's luck is difficult to quantify scientifically. It is, however, a well documented and common fact of life. That it has defied rational investigation may yet again point to an unsympathetic and, therefore, inappropriate system of analysis rather than indicate any real absence of evidence.

To be fair, the subject can be treated on a psychological level. It has been suggested that a rank newcomer is subject neither to the pressure of living up to past performances nor to the tension of trying to achieve a higher standard. Freed from these powerful emotional stresses, the absolute beginner can approach the task with a fluency of mind/body co-ordination that is difficult to reproduce at will.

Traditionally, however, what we know as beginner's luck is inextricably linked with the mysteries of innocence. In its highest form, innocence represents a state of grace where the mystic is freed from the chains of delusion that had held the spirit in a state of captivity. In this liberated condition, there is no hindrance to spontaneity and creativity, and miracles may even occur.

The minor miracle of Tarot cards revealing the future, for instance, can give the reader a first taste of this elevated spiritual state.

Trying to help someone to achieve beginner's luck can be the sheerest folly. Even just describing how this particular brand of luck manifests may rob a person of the complete absence of self-consciousness that is probably its primary characteristic.

This is an intricate subject that cannot be developed fully here. Its application, too, is universal and therefore beyond the confines of this particular book. However, before we leave the subject, we could do worse than consider one important element that does directly correspond to the study of the Tarot.

An adept Tarot reader must be free from the distractions that arise from both hope of success and fear of failure. The interpretation of the cards should not be derived from any preconceptions, bias, or even ideology, but be purely and naturally founded on the present spread. Finally, the message of the cards must be voiced through an open-hearted yearning to be honest, and with all the warmth and enthusiasm to have a go and get on with life. Such is, as we will see in more detail later, precisely the nature of the Fool.

Reading for a client

It is only natural for people to share their interests with others. But in view of the exciting opportunities offered by studying the occult arts, we may wonder why anyone ever consults a Tarot reader. Why don't we all learn to do it for ourselves?

It is a good question. However, the science of genetics teaches us that we cannot all be adept at everything; we need to trust those who are better at things than ourselves. And we need to be able to trust them implicitly. It cannot be stressed often enough that frauds are worse than redundant. They are a danger to themselves.

Most of an honest reader's fears about what can go wrong when interpreting the cards for a client can be summed up with a single example: what do you do when seeing death in the cards?

I do not just mean the particular card with that name. As we will find later, this Trump often signifies metamorphosis or irrevocable change (which may be for the better) rather than physical death. I mean a whole cluster of ominous cards that point inexorably toward catastrophe … Who could calmly state "You're going to die," and go on to say when, where and how?

Unless the client is blind, watching the succession of gloomy and even frightening images on the cards will cause him or her rapidly mounting consternation. Conversation will naturally turn to the subject of fear, loss, and even bereavement. Such circumstances invite the reader to offer counselling and comfort. Please note that the client's personal views, religious or otherwise, must always be respected.

Yet the Tarot actually offers a special avenue of consolation. Because divination functions by virtue of a "supernatural" power, it stands to reason that there is much more to life than our common perception of it on a day-to-day level. Awareness of this additional spiritual layer can often answer a client's anxiety, and bring peace in even the most extreme physical conditions.

That said, even in the most oppressive reading, it is generally beyond the ability of a reader to be 100 per cent certain that the cards actually forecast physical death.

Nevertheless, apart from suggesting a follow-up reading (within a reasonable time frame, of course) the conscientious Tarot reader should carefully advise the client to put his or her affairs in order.

Mostly, people want to hear good things, something they can look forward to with joyful expectancy, which is one reason why popular religions are keen to emphasise the eternal paradise that the faithful can anticipate. So do the cards empower us to transform impending doom into salvation?

Free will

Does prophecy prove that we are all doomed to play out our lives simply to fulfil a fixed fate? At the risk of sounding rhetorical, I would like to answer that question with one of my own: does it really matter?

It is only laziness and pessimism that make the idea of an unalterable fate seem unpleasant. If the future is preordained, and its conclusion inevitable, so what?

We know a great deal about human psychology and the balance of the natural world in which we live. We appreciate what makes us happy and how to sustain a supportive environment. We realise that if we put our minds to something and exercise our will, we can produce prodigious results, even if sometimes it seems that we only attain our heart's desire in spite of our best efforts.

We are all striving to achieve as much as we can. It is a fact of life, a biological imperative. For an increasing number of people, that is sufficient.

Many individuals, though, view our mortal lives as a prelude to (or intermission in) a personal life eternal. For some of these mystics, the matter of free will is essential to their philosophy. For example, without being able to make personal choices, there would be no justice in a jealous God condemning anybody's soul to eternal suffering.

There was a famous legal case in the early twentieth century where the accused argued that he was innocent of any crime because he was purely the product of his environment. To condemn him, he protested, was to punish him for the deficiency of his circumstances. His case failed, however, so the stupendous legal precedent that would have been made did not materialise. Legally, we are still individually responsible for our own actions.

The Tarot, especially the Major Arcana, teaches us about changes, how one thing leads to another. In readings, we can very often see causes arise and with the turning of the next card, witness the effects they have.

The Tarot stresses the importance of taking responsibility for our own lives. Indeed, whether clients know it consciously or not, a vital part of the reason for visiting a Tarot reader is to be given the information that enables them to take control of their lives.

If, at the end of a reading, you feel that you can say to your client, "Look, now you know – it's your responsibility from here on", you have acquitted your own responsibility as a Tarot reader.

Personal integrity

For a client beset with worries and uncertainty, a visit to a Tarot reader can be like stepping out of a crowded and smelly room into warm sunshine and taking a deep breath of fresh air.

Under such circumstances, and given the intimacy of discussing personal matters, it is not surprising that many clients develop an emotional attachment or bond with their Tarot reader.

Many clients take the opportunities afforded to them by divination to "open up" about subjects that are surrounded by social and cultural taboos. Topics include lovers, parents, careers and mental confusion, each of which puts the diviner in a position of power. Some diviners relish this sense of importance, but such emotions can cloud the interpretation, and then all hope of helping the client is doomed to a secular rather than spiritual resolution. However, an open and candid relationship is perfectly natural and to be enjoyed by both parties.

It is a memorable occasion indeed when you first tune in to your client's mind to the extent that you feel the weight your every word carries, sensing every response as it arises in his or her mind. In many ways, this is a form of love. Just as when you are in love you instinctively assume personal responsibility for the welfare of the beloved, the Tarot reader must not abuse this sacred trust. Devotion to the art of divination brings its own rewards.

Preying on clientele is, without doubt, spiritually counter-productive. The use of any magical system for personal advancement over and above the well-being of the client has always been a damnable offence in the lore of the true mysteries.

Occasionally, some clients become somewhat infatuated with their card readers. This phenomenon is well-known in the medical profession, for instance, where patients develop a crush on their doctor, consultant or nurse. Often it is simply the thrill of contact with the supernatural that attracts them, and they mistake their heightened feelings for romance.

In such circumstances, gentle but firm pressure should be used to persuade the client to turn and look elsewhere for the answer to his or her needs. There are numerous groups and societies which are much better equipped than a lone Tarot reader to foster and guide a seeker through the labyrinth of their own self-discovery.

Payment
Most Tarot readings are conducted free of charge. Sometimes this is because the reader simply thinks that occultism should not be used for personal profit. Nevertheless, the ethic of expecting payment for services rendered is so firmly rooted in our society that not charging can seem somehow odd, even subversive.

There are business consultants galore who sell their expertise in areas as diverse as combating computer viruses to buying real estate on the Moon. If these people did not charge for their time, they simply couldn't carry on their livelihood. Is a Tarot reader any different? Do they not need to buy food to eat?

The traditional gypsy fortune-teller takes a pragmatic stance with terms of business clearly stated in advance, saying, "Cross my palm with silver!" Incidentally, silver coins were the smallest denomination in currency for centuries in England and many other European countries. I am sure, too, that "one-off" deals were entered into in order to accommodate people whose meagre income could not afford a single penny. I wonder how many present-day professional fortune-tellers are so versatile.

Incidentally, the colour of silver associates it with the Moon and lunar deities. As moonlight appears to shine most powerfully at night, its symbolic provenance naturally encompasses the unknown mysteries that inhabit the darkness of our ignorance as well as the inner world of our dreams and psychic talents. Such a metal is thus intrinsically appropriate for rewarding services such as divination.

Asking for cash up-front demands that the client trusts the vendor, a possible prerequisite, as we have seen, for the full flowering of those sensitive psychic abilities that enable the complete success of the sitting. But there are no guarantees in divination: the client might not even like the information his or her money buys.

In modern law, the exchange of money for services partakes of the nature of a contract that affords participants certain rights. For example, the service paid for needs to be given and not withheld, and must meet certain reasonable criteria. Likewise, the remuneration should be equal to the task involved.

Normally, the Tarot reader will confine the implicit contract to the act of engaging their attention for the time it takes to read the cards. The information delivered is not explicitly a part of the deal, otherwise the client could potentially sue (through inaccuracy or omission) for damages. If challenged, the diviner can always return the consultation fee and call it quits.

Of course, the legal system in the Western world does not actually recognise magic (and divination falls under this heading), so such contentious legal wrangling would be instantly thrown out of court anyway, but the principle remains as a matter of honour.

In fact, the traditional demand for payment is a form of insurance. By ensuring that the client pays for what is, according to conventional judgement, an absurdity and an irrelevance, the diviner cannot be blamed for gratuitously meddling in someone else's affairs.

By rigidly abiding by the ancient code, a Tarot reader can practise the art without bringing his or her character into question. The payment signifies a bargain struck beyond the pale of rationality – a deal with the Devil, if you will – and one that is utterly unenforceable in law yet irrefutable in concept.

Not only is the receiving of a token a signal to begin a reading, but for the donor it is a gesture of good faith. There are plenty of examples of folk who hand over their entire worldly fortunes to gurus who exemplify their ideals; the investment made by the Tarot reader's client is a trifle in comparison. Nevertheless, the gesture is the important point, for it denotes a sublime acceptance of the message to be received.

Free!

It is, perhaps, only natural for a novice to seek temporarily to reduce the burden of responsibility that all Tarot readers owe their clients.

While you must always judge for yourself whether or when you are ready first to use the cards on behalf of someone else, there are a few guidelines and suggestions that might help to clarify your thoughts.

If you have limited faith in your capacity to read the cards (for whatever reason), you might decide against making any charge for your services. You may even think that what comes for free is reckoned worthless. Think again. The boon of friendship that is implicit in this gift counts for much more in most people's minds than any professional's fee.

Perhaps from the very outset you honestly try to stack the cards in your favour by telling the client that you are doing the reading for free because you're only still a learner. The client will quite possibly be doubly impressed by your obvious sincerity … and this could actually lead him or her to believe your interpretations all the more readily!

Incidentally, to tell a client that you doubt the ability of the cards to reveal anything whilst simultaneously dealing them out is a very curious trick, one open to precious few interpretations, the least flattering of which is that you are a fool.

Usually, a client will go along with the suggestion of "discovering the truth together". The relationship may be further qualified by the simple addition "to the best of our ability". Indeed, such an open policy goes a long way to defusing any pretension and sets a scene that is comfortable and amiable.

This modesty in the attempt to commune with the divine precisely characterises readings by truly accomplished Tarot readers. There is an ancient proverb that says the pupil is one of the teacher's greatest opportunities for learning. Although it can be a bit of a trial, there is no doubt that reading the Tarot for clients offers similar advantages, and can lead to the commencement of a wiser approach to life itself.

3
... and Practice

One of the most fascinating places to start using the cards is by challenging them to answer a question for you. This involves using a spread (a specific way of arranging the cards to read their meanings). There are many different spreads in use around the world; below are detailed four of the most useful and popular.

Few Tarot students confine themselves to purely academic and theoretical research; most wish to put their learning to practical use. I think I may be forgiven, therefore, for making the assumption that you have a Tarot pack handy.

In fact, many students own more than one pack, and regularly use all of them. Because the various packs appeal to and evoke different emotional and mental states, the experienced reader can choose and use the most appropriate pack to answer any particular question.

Please note that in the spreads described, it is traditional, unless otherwise stated, to lay all the cards face downwards, turning over one card at a time and interpreting it first individually and then in the light of preceding cards, if any. The reader must take care to carry the client along with them, and progress together through the spread. A client who gets muddled will not benefit from any advice the cards have to offer. Then, as the final card is turned face up and interpreted, the reader concludes with summing up the whole reading, stressing key points and answering any questions that the client may have.

It is also worth noting here that the cards are often consulted on behalf of someone who is not physically present. Indeed, that person need not even know that they are the subject of a reading. Although this may seem rather like spying, and it certainly demands a more acute sensitivity on the part of the reader, it is common practice and therefore well worth bearing in mind.

Sometimes a client may approach a Tarot reader with a view to discovering something about the prospects of a particular project, such as a business venture. The cards are perfectly capable of answering these queries, and the spreads featured simply need to be read as if the business (or other project) itself is the client.

However, for ease of use, the text detailing the divinatory meanings of each individual card assumes that you are reading the spread for your own benefit. This simply avoids a thousand tedious repetitions of the phrase "the querent"! Of course, the meanings are equally applicable to any querent whatsoever.

Reversed cards

Opinion is divided on whether Tarot cards should have special meaning if they are shuffled so that approximately half the pictures are top to bottom. It is a contentious issue.

Some authorities insist that the Tarot should never be subjected to such ungracious treatment and that the pictures ought to be kept scrupulously the right way up, anything else being tantamount to sacrilege. However, other scholars are much freer in their interpretations and observe that because the cards are physically capable of being seen upside down, they are entitled to have a special metaphysical meaning when reversed.

I could, like many authors, leave the decision up to you. All I would have to do is tell you that a reversed interpretation is basically the same as the ordinary interpretation, except that the force or event will be more difficult, disappointing, inharmonious, unpleasant, mundane, and bitter than otherwise anticipated.

However, I would like to propose what is, to the best of my knowledge, a novel solution. I cannot claim that it is particularly ingenious, but it does benefit from a fundamental simplicity that makes it easy to remember and could therefore have been a part of the original scheme of early Tarot card use.

Broadly speaking, the Major Arcana represent forces that motivate events. They are also envisaged as paths on the Tree of Life. Like people on paths, forces can usually travel to and fro, forwards or backwards, up or down. I would suggest that the Major Arcana should be capable of holding a definite reversed meaning. The Minor Arcana, representing stable events, are less susceptible to this ambiguity.

The icing on the cake for me is that this scheme provides the Tarot pack with precisely 100 possible meanings – and I like round figures! Numerologically, this number is also significant. Raising, as it does, our decimal counting system by a power of 10, it represents not merely the ideas of unity and totality (inherent in 1 and 10) but diversity, progressing exponentially within the whole. It reminds us that we can repeatedly analyse and subdivide the universe into smaller and smaller parts, but the overall and underlying patterns are the same wherever we look. I have, therefore, provided specific reversed meanings for the Major Arcana, and indicated the breadth of the range of meanings for the Minor.

Many readers take their cue from the Major cards as to whether the Minor should be read in their benign, neutral, or malign interpretations. If Major cards are few or entirely absent, then the court cards may provide pertinent clues. Ultimately, this depends on the sensitivity of the reader.

The book

Anyone with even a passing interest in treating the Tarot seriously should consider keeping a diary of their activities.

If divination is going to be a feature of your use of the cards, you should definitely make an effort to keep an accurate record both of what the cards foretell and what came to pass. Do not worry if the results don't seem immediately encouraging, for the diary will help you to take a long-term view. In hindsight, many matters become clear. Trying to see events that have not yet happened is bound to take a little while to learn properly.

Always record your question under a heading containing the date, time, location and any other factors you consider may be relevant – a thunderstorm, colleagues present, etc. Writing it down can even help you spot a poorly chosen or ambiguously phrased question, so wherever practical, record it before consulting the Tarot.

To keep your relationship with the Tarot on a professional basis, be sure to leave plenty of space under your record of each reading where you can write a comparison of the course of events about which you had asked. Incidentally, the spread known as the Cycle is relatively easy to check for evidence of precognition, especially if you use it to forecast the days of the week ahead.

This diary is a very important document. Although the true value of your endeavours to keep it scrupulously accurate might not be immediately apparent, without it you will be infinitely poorer in the long run. Please do not begrudge the short time it takes to set it up ... and keep it up to date.

Setting the scene

Imagine you are going to settle down to a heart-to-heart with a friend. You would probably start thinking about providing drinks, getting rid of any impinging distractions (for example, by switching off the TV, or at least tuning it to a suitable channel), and making yourselves as comfortable as possible.

Now imagine you are going to settle down to consult an ancient and venerable oracle. Any ideas? I mean it. Hold that thought! Your own ideas are likely to be better by far than anyone else's suggestions.

However you feel intuitively that you would like to approach a Tarot reading is probably the best way for you to proceed. The ideas explored here may help you to understand or develop your own preferences, but should not be regarded as necessarily better just because they are traditional. Remember that every tradition started with somebody doing it their way!

Setting the mood for a romantic tête-à-tête is obviously helpful and perfectly normal behaviour. Likewise, taking a little care to make a few preparations is a perfectly natural way to get the most out of a Tarot reading. You certainly do not need an elaborate ritual to help you to contact and commune with the Tarot, although a few people do find it useful for very important readings. Most will benefit from some sort of routine to settle and focus their minds.

However, it should be noted that many people are perfectly happy confining any ritual acts to picking up and shuffling the cards. For them, nothing else is necessary or even advisable. It cannot be stressed enough that following your own instincts (and of course these may change over time) is the most valuable key to a successful consultation.

Clean and tidy

Technically called the Banishing (of evil or unhelpful influences), this initial part of the procedure is designed simply to ensure that there are as few distractions as possible to hinder the consultation. Activities include:

● *Making ready*. If there are distracting sights or sounds from beyond your control, close the windows and curtains, for instance, to block out these disturbances as much as possible.

● *Making room*. The surroundings should be as free from clutter as possible; seeing any such items can trigger distracting thoughts during the reading.

● *Making space*. The place where the cards are to be spread (whether on a table, floor, or wherever) needs to be clean.

● *Bathing and toilet*. To cleanse the body and, symbolically, the mind. Of course, handling the cards with dirty fingers would soon disfigure them.

● *Astral protection*. You may wish to visualise a faint ring of white light, drawn at floor level and encompassing your site. Situate yourself in the middle of this circle, and imagine a tiny sphere of bright light glowing at its precise centre. Concentrate on this orb as it gradually grows larger, ultimately not only filling you (and an equal space below the floor), but also reaching out until its perimeter reaches and infuses the original ring of light.

Conducive atmosphere

Technically termed the Invocation (of beneficial influences), this final stage of preparation is designed to create a focused and invigorating environment in which the consultation can achieve its highest aims. Activities include:

● *Illumination*. You may light a candle. White is traditional, although many people now prefer black (to signify ignorance prior to the reading whose new insight is symbolised by the lighted flame). A single candle may not provide sufficient light to see the cards clearly. In this case, a ritual purist will light the others either directly from the primary candle, or with a splint lit therefrom.

● *Aroma*. Incense or any fragrancer using essential oils or essences (including gem essences) may be employed to add an atmosphere of other-worldliness. The scent is not merely to create a pleasant environment, but to mark the place as special and mystically separate from the ordinary world. Suitable scents include:

+ Sandalwood to banish and protect
+ Myrrh to purify and consecrate
+ Frankincense to aid clairvoyance
+ Cedar to promote all psychic powers.

For more ideas on how to use aroma to stimulate mind, body and spirit, I can recommend a book by my wife, Joules Taylor, *Perfume Power*, scheduled for publication by London House in the year 2000.

● *Talismanic allies.* Any object can possess talismanic powers which, when deliberately brought into play, can help to arouse certain faculties in the Tarot reader. Jewellery makes an unobtrusive and popular vehicle for such psychic powerhouses. Special garments, such as cloaks, have also been popular, although they tend to be seen as overly theatrical by many modern practitioners. The best metal for such talismans is, traditionally, silver. Many contemporary Tarot readers find that certain crystals help to foster their abilities. Crystals (also suitable for making gem essence fragrances) include:

+ Azurite, for enlivening psychic abilities
+ Black opal, for inducing clairvoyance
+ Charoite, for enhancing and empowering psychic abilities
+ Citrine, for promoting psychic awareness
+ Emerald, for gaining the gift of prophecy
+ Morganite, for developing latent psychic abilities
+ Peridot, for practising clairvoyance and prophecy.

For more information about how to use crystals and other minerals for these and other uses, see *Crystals for Health, Home and Personal Power* by Ken and Joules Taylor, published by Collins & Brown in 1999.

● *Invocation.* Any words (whether uttered aloud or recited in the mind alone) that facilitate the reading are helpful. Some are merely intended to focus the reader's mind on the matter in hand, while others call upon pagan deities to grant the reader the gift of the magical art of prophecy. A typical invocation might run: "I am ready to perform divination, the art-out-of-time. May [*name of deity/deities*] guide me in interpreting the ancient symbols that I might learn what is needful for the future benefit of all." Suitable deities include:

+ Hermes, the Greek god versed in occultism
+ Mercury, the Roman god responsible for messages from the gods
+ Odin/Woden, the Teutonic god of shamanic magic and lore
+ Thoth, the Egyptian god of wisdom and magic.

● *Using the Tarot.* Some people prefer to empty their minds when they unwrap and shuffle the cards, allowing the previously induced state of mind to carry them through the shuffling process. Others concentrate with great determination on the subject of the query. Whichever method suits you best is the right one for you.

Tidy and clean

Technically called the Licence to Depart (of beneficial influences), this final part of the procedure is designed simply to wind down the emotionally charged atmosphere and readjust the reader to the ordinary conditions that apply in the everyday world. Activities include:

● *Wrapping up.* Returning the cards to their protective box or wrapping. There is no specific need to shuffle the cards first. Many people simply place the recently used cards at the bottom of the deck.

● *Unwinding.* Reverse whatever actions you took when you began the reading. For example, if you made an Invocation, use a similarly phrased speech to thank them e.g. "As I conclude this divination, I thank [name of deity/deities] for entrusting me with the knowledge that benefits all." If you lit candles or incense, extinguish them in reverse order, finishing with the first one to be lit. If you used the sphere of astral protection, you should visualise the light being drawn back into its centre until it vanishes from mortal perception.

Before beginning ...

Traditionally, the first question you ever ask of the Tarot should be, "Am I ready for you to answer?" This question requires a simple "Yes" or "No" reply, and a single card should serve the purpose.

The spread called The Quick Answer explains the straightforward method of consulting the Tarot in this manner. Incidentally, the subsequent "tips" section refers to more complex situations and is not relevant to this particular question.

You may choose to use any of the ideas already given as a means of tuning-in to the Tarot, but if you feel at all foolish when you are considering one of them, definitely skip it. They are suggested as a guide to popular practice only, not as a series of rules and regulations. Worrying about them can hinder the spontaneity that can be so helpful in Tarot reading. The only one of the suggestions that is strictly necessary, of course, is Using the Tarot, and just applies to shuffling the cards.

Once you have used The Quick Answer, it is vitally important to react sensibly to the answer given. If the card indicates a negative response, do not ignore it and carry on as if nothing had happened. It is important to treat the Tarot with respect, and is as well to start as you mean to go on.

Unfortunately, the Tarot is not particularly good at answering "Yes" or "No". Its strength lies in its ability to tell stories, particularly foretelling events. So this presents us with your first test. (I am assuming that you have not used the cards before.)

When you have found the card that reveals the Tarot's response, you need to determine whether it belongs to the Major Arcana or the Minor Arcana. A list of cards separated into these two categories is provided in the Introduction. Locate and study the relevant text to find your answer.

Some cards are full of occult significance and promise rich attainments (such as the High Priestess, and the Ace of Cups), while others are replete with warnings of doom and failure (such as the Hanged Man, and the 10 of Swords). It is for you to decide whether your card is trying to encourage or discourage you in your attempt to start reading the cards now.

I could give a list of all the cards that would indicate a positive response, but that would deprive you of this valuable opportunity to learn by experience rather than by rote. I think you will thank me in the long run, although you may not feel that way just now!

It might be that even after you have carefully studied the card and its interpretation, you honestly still cannot make up your mind whether it indicates that the Tarot accepts you straight away or not. In these circumstances, you must resist any temptation to plump for the optimistic interpretation. It is far better to defer your decision and, while trying not to suffer the natural feelings of rejection that a "No" answer can give, wait for the Tarot to change its tune.

If you decide that the cards have either declined to answer you clearly or replied with a negative response, you must wait at least until the next day before repeating the question.

Use the time wisely. Familiarise yourself further with the subject, and try to understand the meaning of the card that you drew in The Quick Answer. In particular, attempt to remember any significance that might be found in your dreams. In its use of pictures to convey powerful personal meanings, the Tarot has a strong affinity with dreams.

If, when you try for the second time, the reply is still not sufficiently encouraging to start you confidently using other, more complicated spreads, you must reconsider your position once again. This time, wait for two days before you ask the same question again. In fact, for every occasion that it fails to give you a welcoming signal, you should add an additional extra day before trying again.

Do not think of any such delay in terms of outright rejection. During this time, you can study any aspect of the Tarot whatsoever, excepting only that you should refrain from using any spreads, even The Quick Answer. Some people find such a wealth of meaning in the other uses of the Tarot (notably the Tarot Mysteries) that they do not concern themselves with divination at all. Is this the message the Tarot is offering to you? Perhaps it is something completely different: maybe you would do better to concentrate on other matters first (such as examinations, your career, a special relationship, etc.) rather than start studying a new and absorbing subject just now.

You must try to find the reason for its continuing negative answer, then you have the best chance of satisfying the Tarot that you are at last ready to begin to learn the practice of divination.

Incidentally, some people might think that the law of averages demands that sooner or later you will receive a "Yes" card. It is foolish to place your hope in such frivolous and flimsy ideas. For example, every time you toss a coin there is a 50 per cent chance of it falling as heads. But the laws of probability have no memory, and there is nothing to stop it falling heads every time you toss it for as long as you live. Instead, treat the probationary period with respect. The reasons for the delay may not appear immediately obvious, but they should have your own best interests at heart, so do not despair.

As soon as the go-ahead is received, it is likely that you will want to try one of the other spreads. The choice is yours, but I would recommend something relatively straightforward, such as the Cycle.

In time, you should try as many spreads as you can; each has something special to offer. Especially if you are going to conduct a reading for a client, you ought to be familiar enough with them all to be able to choose the particular spread that will answer the given query most comprehensively.

As you gain experience, you may find that given a particular question you could devise a new spread that would provide a better (which is to say, more appropriate) answer than any of the illustrated examples. Do not be afraid of adding your own ideas to the Tarot, for this is how it grows and evolves. Like anything else, without constant development and upgrading, the Tarot would have become obsolete and extinct long before now.

It is always worth remembering, too, that any reading can be abandoned if difficulties in interpreting it are insurmountable. Sometimes the cards seem to think we are better off not knowing and do everything in their power to remain utterly opaque and inscrutably silent. In such circumstances, discretion is definitely the better part of valour.

At other times, we are simply too tired to complete a complex reading, but take care not to admit defeat too often. Then, the cards should be left in their places until you are refreshed. If it is impractical to leave them *in situ*, at least make a written record. The important point is to return as soon as possible to complete your interpretation of the reading.

However, when the cards seem willing to co-operate, and you are far from exhausted but just cannot figure out one particular part of a sequence, the Quick Answer can be a real psychic eye-opener.

The Quick Answer

Sometimes, all we need is a one-word answer to show us how we stand. The Tarot is perfectly capable of dealing us that hand.

Simply shuffle the cards thoroughly, taking care not to see the card on the bottom of the pack. This is the card bearing the most important message that the Tarot has for you at this time. When you are content that you have shuffled sufficiently, turn up the card and read the response.

Tips

If you are using the Quick Answer to clarify the meaning of another spread, do not shuffle the pack before selecting a card. We must place our trust in the Tarot and assume that it always knew that you would get stuck.

We can presume that it has already very obligingly positioned the precise card you need right on top of the pack (not at the bottom, as with a one-off Quick Answer reading). All you have to do is steel your nerves and turn it over. Hey presto! There is the answer for which you were looking.

If this does not work, it is probably advisable to postpone or even abandon the confusing reading. It might also be wise to take a break. In rare cases it is permissible to seek another Quick Answer to shed light on the first, but it is imprudent (some might say impudent) to read more than three successive Quick Answers on the same subject.

The Cycle

This is perhaps the best known of all spreads. It is also very versatile and powerful, yet requires little effort to construct or interpret.

The full title of this spread is One Cycle of the Spiral, a name that dispels any worries about dreary repetition or lack of progress going around in vicious circles. Rather, it wholeheartedly embraces the concept of evolution and perpetual change.

It is almost unrivalled in its simplicity when used to foresee the future. *Figure 1* shows the spread with twelve cards in a circle. Each card represents one month, so the whole spread reveals the year ahead. The central card illustrates the general character of the entire cycle (in this case, the year ahead). It may also reveal a particular

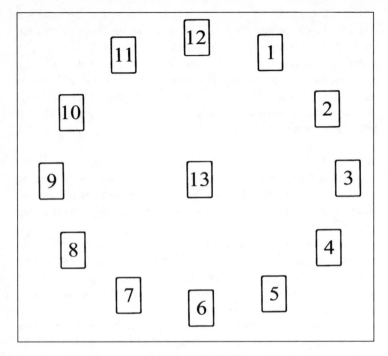

Figure 1. The Cycle

lesson that needs to be addressed and learned in order to avoid making mistakes in the following cycle.

It is usual to start laying down the cards as shown, as if on a clock face where the one o'clock position represents the first month of the reading. In this case, twelve o'clock represents the situation in exactly twelve months' time.

However, the amount of time that the Cycle foresees is up to you. Instead of twelve cards in the circle, you may use seven – one for each of the days of the forthcoming week, plus a central card to summarise the whole week. Follow the same clockwise pattern when you lay the cards down (the Cycle will be completed by eight instead of thirteen cards) so that the card at the top represents the same day of the week as that upon which the reading takes place.

Although it is possible to use the Tarot cards to foresee each of the forthcoming 52 weeks of the year, it is scarcely practical as the spread is likely to be some two metres wide! If this degree of detail is required, you should use a series of consecutive spreads, shuffling the cards after every layout. Each could show the weeks in a month, or even the weeks in a season.

A spread for each day of the forthcoming month is sometimes used, although even this is likely to have a spread of an unwieldy size. But experiment for yourself. Feel free to use this spread for any period of time about which you wish to learn.

Tips

Divination of one sort or another has always been particularly popular during New Year celebrations. The Cycle is a perfect spread for New Year's Eve. Tarot readers can easily find themselves the centre of attention for hours if they are unwise enough to carry a pack to a party!

Samhain – or Hallowe'en as it is commonly called – is the ancient Celtic New Year festival, and is still strongly associated with the supernatural. On that night the barrier between our world and the spirit realms is believed to become tenuous and easily penetrated, making it perfect for prophecy of all sorts. You may also choose to use the Celtic lunar calendar for this particular reading, whereby each card relates to one lunar month (usually reckoned from new moon to new moon). Therefore, to complete a whole year, you will need a traditional spread of 13 cards.

Almost everyone who starts reading the cards does so by referring to the text related to the cards in the spread. However, by degrees, as memory takes the place of cribbing, the imagination begins to exert a subtle effect. With perseverance, links and relationships between the cards of the spread begin to appear before the mind's eye.

This spread tells a straightforward story: one card leads inexorably to the next. Just as the seasons are all clearly distinct from each other, the cards can present wildly different pictures side by side. Remember that on a day-to-day level, the seasons often blend imperceptibly into one another. It is the reader's task to find this middle ground.

Every student must learn to read between the cards. It is the learned skill of the experienced reader that bridges the gap between the textual divinatory meaning of the adjacent cards. Only then can the reader present the querent with a coherent story line that is easy to follow and understand, and from which they may derive benefit.

Some students appear to master this technique very quickly, particularly people with an interest in creative writing and/or music. Others struggle and stumble, and are sometimes utterly unable to find a plausible link between two apparently contradictory cards.

These suffering students should not think themselves unfortunate or handicapped because, as is so often the case in occult study, an apparent difficulty veils a valuable opportunity. Whereas people who are fluent in using their imagination may become content with using this ability to find an easy answer, those who strive in the gulf of not-knowing might find that their intuition and psychic abilities (rather than merely their imagination) blossom to fill the void. In either instance, practice makes perfect!

The Houses of the Heavens

This spread uses the ancient tradition of the astrological houses, the twelve compartments that encompass every aspect of our lives.

The twelve Houses contain all the various activities and situations we encounter during our day-to-day lives. It is for this reason that this spread offers an unparalleled holistic view of the client and their current circumstances.

The cards are laid out in the same sequence as the Houses (see *Figure 2*).

The First House is the House of the Self. It represents egocentric interests, and includes self-image and instinctive reactions to daily situations and other people. It also represents new beginnings of all sorts.

Cards lying in this House indicate purely personal matters and can reveal intimate aspects of behaviour. In questions concerning relationships, this House can indicate the physical type of the other person.

In matters of health, while a reading cannot and should not presume to replace qualified medical advice, the card in this position

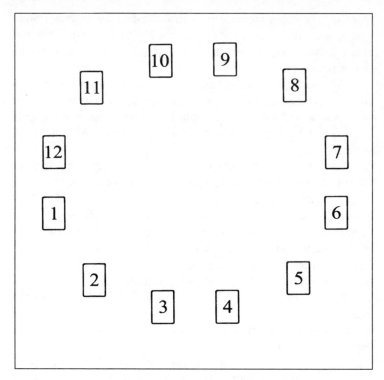

Figure 2. Houses of the Heavens

might both indicate possible avenues of investigation, and serve as a guide when considering preventative measures.

The Second House is the House of Personal Resources. This House relates to personal possessions, money from sources other than employment, acquisitive abilities, and the discovery of latent talents. Especially, it governs earning and spending, and power based directly on personal skills and business acumen as opposed to work or career.

. Cards in this position indicate particular personal qualities that may need to be brought to bear (or avoided) in order to resolve a particular question under enquiry.

The Third House is the House of Communication. This House highlights relationships with the immediate environment, especially with siblings, acquaintances and neighbours.

Cards here can indicate ways to facilitate easy communication with these people in order to help to resolve problems. They can also relate to your own mental development and relationship with the material universe.

The Fourth House is the House of the Home. It encompasses a person's base of operations, the local environment within which we operate and exercise our abilities. It particularly represents parents and parental influence, the home itself and the home environment.

Cards in this House position can also give insight into the root causes of behavioural problems and disruptive tendencies.

The Fifth House is the House of Creative Self-Expression. This reveals your ability and scope for establishing yourself in the world at large. Children (of either mind or body), pets, hobbies, social life, love affairs, and the pursuit of recreation and pleasure are all included.

Cards lying here may even suggest new avenues of self-expression, or indicate the tenor of intimate relationships.

The Sixth House is the House of Service. This House reveals the efficiency with which you function within the community. It covers the quality and quantity of co-operation that exist between yourself and society in general.

In particular, cards here can show your emotional attitude to work as well as your effectiveness within the work place.

The Seventh House is the House of Relationships. The concern here is with partnerships of all kinds. It deals particularly with those of marriage and the long-term personal partner.

Business partnerships are also contained in this House, as are open enemies (the results of failure to achieve harmonious relationships with others).

Cards in this position can provide insight into what to expect from your current or long-term relationships.

The Eighth House is the House of Shared Resources. It is concerned with money itself rather than the ability to earn it, especially jointly held or corporate money, and inheritances.

It is also deeply concerned with spiritual or occult matters and experimentation.

Perhaps because it is often necessary to sacrifice one's personal interests for the sake of the community, the Eighth House is also known as the House of Death. As with the Tarot card Death, indications of death can be symbolic of the completion of a cycle, the passing-away of a phase, or simply irrevocable change. The reader should pay particular attention to the voice of intuition when interpreting these messages.

The Ninth House is the House of Distant Horizons. It is concerned with increasing awareness, and the desire to experience life to the full. This House describes the ways in which these urges may best be put into action, and can be particularly helpful when you are facing a crisis.

It encompasses a range of fields, including philosophical matters, higher education, law, religion and travel.

Cards lying here can indicate appropriate attitudes and responses for situations encountered in the wider arena of life, and/or give a warning of what to avoid.

The Tenth House is the House of Status. It deals specifically with your position in the community, generally with the consolidation of career ambitions, and the attainment of prestigious social achievement.

Cards here can suggest whether to expect favour or disfavour from those in authority, and offer some pertinent advice. They may also indicate possible new avenues for career progression.

The Eleventh House is the House of Communal Expression. It deals with the achieving of ideals for and within a group or community. It also describes your circle of friends and/or acquaintants, humanitarian hopes and wishes, and can indicate by what method these aspirations may be achieved.

Cards in this position might suggest values and virtues that you can bring to the community, ways of directly improving society, and the sorts of friends to seek out (or avoid) in order to achieve your own hopes and dreams within the aegis of the community.

The Twelfth House is the House of Integration. This House reveals the ending of particular phases of life, preparatory to new beginnings.

Cards here indicate forthcoming changes in your life. They tend to portray emotional responses to life, especially the fulfilment (or collapse) of hopes and wishes. They can also reveal limitations and self-undoing.

This House is also closely connected with the unconscious mind, the development of intuitive or psychic abilities, and psychological health.

It is worth noting that, generally speaking, the first six Houses are characterised by personal or subjective factors – e.g. personal resources (House Two), whereas Houses Seven through to Twelve deal primarily with situations that do not directly revolve around you (or the client), but are of an objective or impersonal nature, such as shared resources (House Eight).

In fact, the astrological tradition maintains that there is a form of celestial symmetry that reflects House One into House Seven, Two into Eight, and so forth around the entire circle.

Tips

Note: the layout of this spread may appear similar to that of the Cycle of twelve cards, but is subtly different. The position of the first card and the direction of subsequent placement are, of course, completely different.

The Houses provide a snapshot of your whole life. We are all prone to getting wrapped up in a particular issue to the extent that we tend to ignore other facets of our lives. This spread helps us to understand the big picture.

It is, therefore, an ideal spread to use when clients need counselling, are taking stock of their lives, or face a challenge that will need all their strength and resources to meet.

Usually, the Houses are used to portray the situation at the present time. However, an experienced reader can set his or her mental clock to any point in the future (or past). This spread will then provide a picture of that particular time.

The Celtic Cross

This spread is particularly popular because not only does it forecast the future, but specifically identifies obstacles along the way.

Perhaps because it is so popular, there are a number of slight variations on how to lay the cards. Nevertheless the Positions are generally consistent in their meanings. The spread described here (see *Figure 3*) is arguably the most natural and, therefore, the easiest way of answering your needs.

Position 1. You (or, of course, the client). This card acts rather like a mirror, revealing you to yourself – interpreting this card for a client

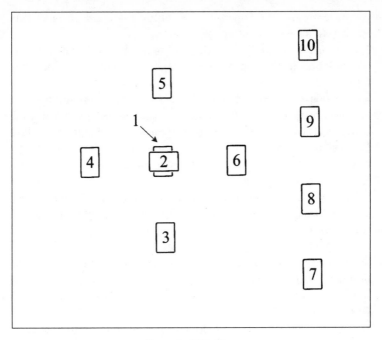

Figure 3. Celtic Cross

might call for a degree of tact! – and shows the personal character-istics that are currently most significant. It can also indicate the conditions currently surrounding you.

Position 2. The Opposition. This card indicates the obstacles that are preventing you from achieving the goals that are currently being pursued. Never read the 'reversed' meaning for this card.

Position 3. Past Guidance. Here are revealed the influences that have shaped the current situation. Included are the effects that friends and other people have had. Sometimes these influences have roots that stretch into childhood and beyond.

Position 4. Past Events. The recent past is depicted. Obviously, as only a single card can occupy this Position, the entire corpus of events is usually symbolised as a single image that characterises the most significant occurrence or trend.

Position 5. Future Guidance. Occasionally, these are a direct continuation of those depicted at Position 3. Often though, matters will have progressed. Sometimes, an entirely new set of forces can be seen to have come into play.

Position 6. Future Events. The card here depicts the character of the situation in the short-term. It must be remembered that this represents a phase that will come to pass.

Position 7. The Self. We are all full of potential. Certain events in our lives bring out specific strengths and/or weaknesses. The card here reveals which are to be brought to the fore as the future unfolds.

Position 8. The Group. This represents your family, friends, or colleagues, etc. These form the present environment that is influencing your actions or intentions.

Position 9. Hope and Fear. Traditionally, if the card here is generally beneficial, it represents your hopes. If detrimental or malefic, your fears are revealed.

Position 10. Consequences. The card here depicts the character of situation in the long-term, and reveals the outcome to the question that you have asked.

Tips

When using this spread, it is helpful to phrase your question in such a way as to indicate a time scale. In this way, the cards that depict the near and long-term future can be interpreted to a greater level of satisfaction and accuracy.

Position 2 needs a little extra consideration. It shows obstacles to your goals. We would rightly expect that for anyone with worthy aspirations, the card that falls here represents an enemy of love and liberty. However, in many readings the card falling here depicts a beneficial subject. But how do we interpret this? Simply by realising that there is a grave flaw in your good intentions. Again, this may demand a tactful interpretation: some clients might honestly be unaware that their ambitions are detrimental to everyone but themselves!

Such instances of positively salubrious cards blocking destructive ambitions can be difficult to interpret in a way that a client will accept. If handled sympathetically, this message can induce a very significant (if not positively remarkable) change of heart.

In a sense, the adept reader can become the mouthpiece of the card that is opposing a client's mistaken ambition. If the reading is completely successful, the client no longer has to suffer living through the obstacle as it plays out in his or her life, for it will have been cleared in the space of the reading itself. If such a reading is for yourself, you may learn much of the ineffable value of the Tarot in one fell swoop. This single instance ably demonstrates the potential benefits of this spread in particular and Tarot reading in general.

Obviously, much can depend on the turning of the last card. It is always important for you to put situations into context. Without undermining the effectiveness of the reading, it is wise to remember that truth that lies in the traditional identification of Tarot with ROTA, the Wheel (of Fortune). To put it crudely, life is full of ups and downs. Learn to deal with every eventuality wisely ... and you will never be the loser.

4

The Minor Arcana

Disks

This suit represents the earthy, physical elements of life. In many Continental Tarot packs this suit is called Money or Coins, which emphasises its relevance to the mundane day-to-day life that we all share. Often it indicates the condition of your career, but equally can reveal aspects of the home.

If a spread exhibits a preponderance of Disks, the focus of the reading should be on practical issues and hard facts. This is not to say that Disks lack subtlety or are uninspiring. On the contrary, Disks signify not only the natural world and all its wonders, but the full range of human circumstance. If most of the cards are unfavourable, the querent is particularly warned against the pitfall of gross materialism.

According to some modern thinking (a position ardently proposed by Aleister Crowley), the Disks should not be imagined as static two-dimensional objects, but as whirling orbs of concentrated energy. Perhaps we should briefly consider the concept of the chakra as described in ancient Indian mystical philosophy. These bodily energy centres are variously represented as open lotus blossoms and as spinning wheels. However, in the rarefied atmosphere of profound contemplation, the yogi finds that these apparently conflicting ideas merge and provide a unique insight into the complexity and illusory character of appearances.

Ace of Disks

The physical body, the matter in hand, the raw materials that lie inert yet contain unlimited potential, latent talents, security, stability, solidity, inertia, resistance to change, reliability.

This card can be read with meanings as diverse as building a firm foundation for future growth, and reaching rock bottom after a decline in fortunes (much depends on associated cards).

It is identified with the alchemical lapis philosophorum, the "philosopher's stone" that cures any malady, transmutes base metals into gold, and brings ultimate wisdom. The Ace of Disks is a touchstone of reality that dispels ignorance, and disillusions the gullible. It is a mandala (meaning "disk" in Sanskrit) that contains within itself all the secrets of the universe, and yet is intrinsically worthless in the eyes of the uninitiated.

This Ace can also mean money and all the various elements of home, comfort, status and security that cash can buy (all coins are, symbolically, building blocks). It might also be suggesting that you make a conscious attempt to get back to nature and re-establish the link with the Earth that modern civilisation has chronically weakened.

Two of Disks

Change, movement, fluctuating fortunes, perturbation, alteration, ebb and flow, changing tides, new interests, and turning your back on the obsolete, contradictions, exciting news.

"All things change" is the only unchanging rule of life. Embrace this concept now or be left behind in the backwaters of evolution. The rather trite saying "As one door closes another opens" is perhaps better expressed here as "For every hilltop gained a new horizon presents itself to your gaze". It may be wise to seek a position of equilibrium in the midst of change; thereby is inner harmony achieved.

It is vital not to despise (through your own lack of understanding) the old, weak, or enfeebled, for in the fullness of time you may come to share their point of view. This card contains much of the symbolism of the ancient Yin-Yang emblem of Chinese philosophy.

The incessant rising and falling of the ocean tides, like our own breathing, symbolise rising hopes and inspiration, and relaxation and letting go respectively. This card simply shows that there are two conflicting foci of attention (or gravity wells) that are mutually exclusive. Associated cards in the spread indicate which one lies in your future and which will be consigned to the past.

Three of Disks

Work, building, construction, renovation, industry, crafts, manual labour, employment, striving to achieve a concrete goal.

This card symbolises new projects, especially business ventures. The raw materials are at hand, so now is the time to put your talents to use. Whether a quick fix or a prolonged labour of love, the emphasis must now be on working hard to realise (i.e. make real) cherished ideas and dreams.

Sometimes an honest stint of hard physical labour will work like a charm to dispel a host of mental anxieties. It can also provide a good deal of personal satisfaction, and build a good reputation, even fame.

The focus here is to get in touch with your physical body and channel your energies through your capabilities. In a sense, it scarcely matters what you are working towards (it could be as much a hobby as a career), so long as you are actively creating something that everyone can see and touch. Preferably, too, it should be able to withstand the test of time and be admirable for its beauty as well as its function.

Four of Disks

Establishment, consolidation, power-base, security, strength, achievement, independence, maturity, self-defence, a fortress, wealth.

This card indicates that instead of initiating new ventures or instituting radical changes, the achievements to date should now be carefully stabilised and protected. Once the gains are quantified and safeguarded, the fruits of past labour can be enjoyed in peace and without fear of loss through negligence of over-ambition.

Prosperity is assured, and control over your surroundings is achieved through consensus and negotiation rather than coercion or force.

At the heart of this card is the concept of law and order, accepted voluntarily and instituted with a mandate from the masses. This card also represents strength in numbers, and proposes the benefits (and personal limitations) of being part of a powerful group.

Five of Disks

Risk, gambling, equal prospects of causing great loss or making worth-

while gains, worry, anxiety, indecision in the face of the necessity for action, instability.

The problem here is that opportunities are slipping away all the while that you remain uncommitted to a single strategy. You are confronted with the unknown: there seems no way to predict the outcome of the decisive action that the situation demands. If no positive steps are taken, the inevitable result will be stagnation and further degradation of personal resources. For example, in an extreme case this card can signify bankruptcy.

A stubborn streak that hobbles the imagination can also be indicated. Despair is a luxury that cannot be afforded. Although hope may not yet be in sight, it is still possible for you to change direction and find a new source of comfort and well-being.

This card also represents being stuck in a rut. Sometimes, the action that is called for in order to escape the present course is the deliberate leaving behind of cherished but unsupportable habits, routines, ideas, and even colleagues. It can also be a time for discovering new friends who have also suffered profound disappointment and reversals in life.

Six of Disks
Well-being, health, minor but significant triumphs, success of a particular venture, constructive stability, robust dealings with the outside world, solvency.

This is a time for rest after struggling to arrive at a satisfactory conclusion or plateau. The chances of your current attainments disintegrating are slim, and in any case equally balanced by your personal energy. This is a time to be positive and objective, to deal even-handedly with all and sundry, and to be patient to enjoy the fruition of your dreams. However, take note, for this situation is inevitably impermanent, so do not neglect your duties to yourself and loved ones.

At its heart, this card indicates sharing and the redistribution of wealth. This is an on-going process in which we all participate both as giver and receiver. This card shows that the scales are currently balanced and that giving is now as important as getting. This has a special meaning for those involved in an intimate, or especially, a romantic relationship.

Seven of Disks

Hazard, negligence, avoidable peril, castles built on sand, failure, investments swept away at a single stroke, hard but unprofitable work, the grievous legacy of imprudence.

It is time to be alert to the possibility of misfortune. Anyone caught sitting on their laurels will be severely dealt with. Inaction now allows the legacy of past efforts to be squandered and lost. Inertia at a time of imminent threat is not just senseless, but an open invitation to disaster.

This is a particularly bad time to have all your eggs in one basket. Diversification is recommended in order to reduce dependence and risk in any one sector. This is especially applicable to financial and career matters.

This is also a general warning that whatever is planted in poisoned soil will, perhaps despite initial appearances, inevitably bear nothing but bitter fruit. Beware of entering into financial arrangements and political commitments that ultimately betray your own integrity, your loved ones, or your world.

Eight of Disks

Skill, adroit use of personal resources, perspicacity, objectivity, perseverance, prudence, humility, applied intelligence, employment.

Putting common sense to good use is the key to a steady rise in fortunes. It is useless possessing the wit and insight to know what ought to be done without also having the self-discipline to pursue the course that wisdom dictates. The fusion of a sound theoretical knowledge with the practical skill necessary to undertake the task is the hallmark of success.

This card indicates a situation that is supportive of further development. Business growth and financial gain are both possible if additional effort is applied to matters already in hand.

The simple pleasures in life are sufficient to nurture the spirit when the mind and body are working in harmony towards a secure future. The sense of contentment that infuses such agreeable labour not only heartens the immediate family, but extends a beneficial influence into the community at large. Many minor quarrels may now be settled amicably.

Nine of Disks

Opportunities, gifts received, boons, offerings and promises which can be taken at face value, nature's bounty, luxury, prosperity, growth, order out of chaos.

As if a cornucopia has been emptied at your feet, there are riches within easy reach. Effort is no longer needed for progress to be made. Similarly as if from nowhere, life is showering you with presents.

Unexpected good fortune and an increase in worldly belongings are indicated by this card. It represents the vista that suddenly opens out before you when you attain the summit of a hill. This is the time to consider which path you will travel. Many are open to you, but there is no immediate urgency to spoil your deliberations. Enjoy the freedom of choosing your future. Relax, but stay alert. After all, you do not want to overlook even the tiniest possibility, for it might be a gem.

Business ideas and career plans coming to fruition not only bring material wealth, but afford the luxury of considering many further ventures. Possibilities are multiplied at every step.

Ten of Disks

Abundance, wealth, prosperity, security, safety, relaxation, home life, indulgence, plenitude, advantage, privilege, nurture.

Here, what was begun long ago has not simply been achieved, but now provides the secure foundation for a new generation to begin their own journey of growth. Every advantage is offered. The stage is set and replete with props. Now the characters can take their places and make the most of the ample opportunities that are within their reach.

Influential ancestors, family traditions, legacies and other matters of historical importance, as well as your own domestic situation, are all indicated by this card. Apart from family ties, a strong influence being exerted by close friends is also represented here.

Underlying this card is the idea that physical wealth is absolutely worthless and inert unless somebody can use it to create the optimum conditions for family life to thrive. Money needs to be thoroughly composted before it can become the rich soil in which a love may germinate and liberty flourish.

Princess of Disks

This young woman is sensible, careful, thrifty, diligent, well-organised, methodical, and enjoys routine and stability in her life. A keen student, her actions are conscientious, and as far as her relative inexperience will allow, above reproach. Her feet are firmly planted on the ground. Possessed of above average physical strength, she can also be stubborn.

In romance, she may be slow to show her feelings, but is capable of deep passion and intense loyalty.

Metaphorically, this card can represent a new or fledgling business venture, or new course of study. It may also advise that her character traits are/should be uppermost in your own mind, or be a warning against materialism, pomposity, inconsistency, lethargy and jealousy.

Prince of Disks

This young man is conventional, patient, persevering, reliable, cautious, and capable of tremendous endurance. While fond of leisure, he is also always ready to be of service. Honour, loyalty and faithful friendship are natural to him. Practical responsibilities rest lightly on his broad shoulders. He is slow to anger, but implacable if roused. In romance, he is kindly, faithful and warm, and provides security.

Metaphorically, this card can represent a business venture that has not long been established or is branching into a new field. It may also indicate a course of study which, although begun, is less than half way through. It might also advise that his character traits are/should be uppermost in your own mind, or be a warning against deceit, resentment, complacency and subterfuge.

Queen of Disks

This mature woman is generous, magnanimous, profound, sensible, hard-working, stable, and appreciative of the good things of life. Her love of luxury and instinctive appreciation of how to make people feel relaxed and at home make her, among other aspects, a munificent and accommodating hostess.

In romance she is affectionate, sensuous, and is happy with herself, her life and her sexuality.

Metaphorically, this card can represent a business venture that has overcome its growing pains and lost some of its original vigour. This loss is, however, more than compensated for by an increasingly practical approach to sustainable industry. It may also indicate a course of study that is enjoyed for its own sake rather than for any hope of benefits that completion and/or qualifications could bring. It might also advise that her character traits are/should be uppermost in your own mind, or be a warning against servility, flattery, extravagance and self-satisfaction.

King of Disks

This mature man is laborious, practical, down to earth, deeply fond of nature, and possessed of generosity and common sense. His sense of natural justice makes him slow to anger but, if provoked to act, his judgement can be Earth-shattering in intensity.

He is at the height of his powers and has achieved high status through a combination of hard work, patience, and a fundamental honesty of character that has gained him support and popularity.

In romance, he is characteristically sensual, and truly likes and respects women for themselves rather than what they can do for him.

Metaphorically, this card can represent a business venture that is at the height of its success. It may also indicate a course of study that is reaching its natural culmination. It might also advise that his character traits are/should be uppermost in your own mind, or be a warning against rank materialism, avarice, conceit, selfishness, and an inability to see beyond the attractions of the instant gratification of carnal desires.

Swords

This suit symbolises the intellect, intelligence, and the use of our powers of discrimination and judgement. Justice and the legal system are also key features of the rational approach to life exemplified by this suit. Obviously, the way we think and use our minds has a great impact on every aspect of our daily lives. These are explored in the following cards. If a spread has a preponderance of Swords, the main emphasis of the reading lies in your state of mind, and can indicate a period of critical self-examination. Perhaps fresh ideas are being brought sharply into focus, or a new and broader awareness is dawning. If the cards are mostly unfavourable, you face a time of destructive criticism, possibly from yourself.

Swords are traditionally associated with pain and disruption, perhaps because historically the conflict between ideologies has rarely been settled entirely peaceably. Indeed, the amount of strife caused by what are essentially mere differences of opinion is heart-breaking, especially when you consider the wars and persecution caused by conflicting religious beliefs – beliefs that originally offered their subjects a vision of eternal peace and security, but paradoxically betrayed those simple hopes.

Ace of Swords
The mind, thought, consideration, intellect, intelligence, analysis, judgement, discrimination, decision.

The inner battle between opposing ideas, and mental struggle to arrive at a decision are indicated here. This Ace signifies the process itself. It does not offer any advice as to which side should prevail, but strongly suggests that a dedicated effort be made to think matters through carefully, methodically and completely. A cool head and alert mind are called for.

If full and unbiased consideration is devoted to the quandary, this card assures us that even against apparently overwhelming odds, we will prevail, achieve our aims, and enjoy a bright future. It may well be that this process will be characterised by a time of upheaval and change, but through justice and wisdom, eventual triumph is traditionally affirmed.

The full might of the legal system is also depicted by this card. With it comes a possible warning that unless you take control of your own affairs and make the correct choice, the problem may escalate to the stage where matters are decided by an independent arbiter, possibly even the law itself.

Two of Swords
Stasis, balance, equilibrium, ambiguity, contradiction, immobility, inactivity, impasse, rest, poise, self-control, peace.

79

Two opposing ideas have fought to a standstill. Much may already have been lost in the struggle, but now the two sides are in deadlock, and no further progress for either party is possible. Only the passage of time and the intervention of an outside force can free the combatants. For now, the waiting game must be endured. This process might strengthen relationships between colleagues. Friendships rooted in common suffering may easily outlast these present troubles.

This card does not indicate whether the lull in the conflict will culminate in the problem being solved amicably, or if active hostilities will eventually be renewed.

Three of Swords

Pain, suffering, heartbreak, confusion, sorrow, grief, destitution, dismay, loss, discord, destruction, defeat, disaster.

The sword divides. It separates lovers, communities and countries. It sunders hope from the heart, and brings death to dreams. Even when used creatively and for the greater good, the sword is an instrument of trauma, bringing shock and anguish to those on the sharp end of its plying.

It often announces the sudden reversal of previous good fortune. Disappointment, disruption and alienation are all signified by this card. The monstrous actions of secret enemies may also be indicated. Although the clouds of despair that bear tears like rain could, one day, turn out to have a silver lining, this prospect is not yet apparent.

Four of Swords

Relaxation, respite, truce, intermission, cessation from labour, a pause in the fighting, a time to regroup, recuperation.

A meeting of minds has brought a halt to violent struggle. The conditions for dialogue and negotiation have been achieved, and there is a resolve on all parts to settle problems through consensus rather than war. However, there has been no outright winner. The seeds of future conflict remain fertile, so it is prudent to be vigilant despite the overtures of peace.

Paradoxically, it may take the threat of force and even some display of strength of arms to arrive at a peaceful settlement. The prospect of a return to the full horror of war can sometimes help to concentrate the protagonists' minds, persuading them not lightly to abandon the peace process.

This card signifies a period of compromise. Here, convention holds sway over radical ideas. It indicates the establishment of a modicum of calm in the midst of chaos.

Five of Swords

Defeat, downfall, failure, disgrace, loss, decline, degradation, humiliation, diminution, reduction, downsizing, reversal.

At a stroke the goal is lost, ambition is thwarted, and the end is come. This is defeat, not death, so life continues, but it must now learn to do without everything it gambled, for those things are truly lost. It remains only to accept the unavoidable and surrender gallantly to a future definitely not of your own choosing.

There is wisdom in analysing the battle and learning from the weaknesses or vagaries that allowed the course of the conflict to turn against you. However, it is obviously counter-productive to dwell overly much on the past when the future needs so much attention, now more so than before.

Six of Swords

Understanding, minor enlightenment, purposeful and accurate thinking, self-confidence, overcoming obstacles, progress, travelling forward in safety.

By gathering all the facts, examining them carefully, and relating them to each other as if they were pieces in a jigsaw, you will be able to move out of danger.

This card advises that even (or especially) somebody who prefers a spontaneous and haphazard way of life should focus on the matter in hand in a systematic fashion. The scientific approach of considering simple causes and their effects will shed so much light on the situation that the only way to avoid slipping into trouble will become clear.

Traditionally, this card can signify a physical journey to a different environment as well as a departure from outmoded habits into a new way of thinking.

Seven of Swords

Lack of control, losing grip, missing out, wasted effort, missing the point, being off target, turning your back, futility, despair.

It is as if the very forces of nature are combining to deny you happiness. Circumstances beyond your control appear orchestrated to thwart your every move. Despite taking as many precautions as you possibly could, the most implausible occurrences seem to be finding and penetrating every little chink in your armour.

Collectively, their effect is devastating and will ensure your prospects are far from rosy. It may be advisable to accept your losses and move in a new direction. However, at such an unfavourable time as this, even this action may prove ultimately useless or counterproductive.

At this point, every concession will be seized upon as a sign of vulnerability, and the attack intensify against you. The only way forward is through cunning, lateral thinking, and the tactics of indirect attack. Even outright subterfuge is traditionally recommended if this card appears in a spread revealing other malefic forces ranged against you.

Eight of Swords

Restriction, limitation, being tied up in red tape, interference, pedantry, obsession, compulsion, nit-picking, stuffiness, hypocrisy, intellectual narcissism.

Here, logic imposes impossible constraints on natural behaviour. Too much thinking and not enough feeling disrupts day-to-day life. The natural scheme of things has been analysed to the extent where everything is being taken out of context and no longer makes sense: it is broken. Self-discipline through linear thinking has usurped honest emotions. Rules have replaced love.

In the darkness of this exile of the soul, it is unnecessary (perhaps even unwise) to seek to return to nature. In due course, the sun of natural life will inexorably rise of its own accord, thawing the frigid mind and freeing its captive. Patience now will be rewarded with slow but steady progress.

Nine of Swords

Nightmare, horror, fear of the unknown, mental cruelty, fright, terror, irrational fear, phobia, depression, morbidity, woe.

Knowledge of the facts of life (especially the inevitability of death) can bring disquiet to the most tranquil soul. With unaccountable coincidence and almost surreal circumstance, a bolt of disaster may fall from a clear blue sky. When it does, there is little in our homespun philosophies that can comfort the terrified and afflicted.

Time, it is said, cures all. The memory of pain, however, and the loss of emotional security that victims experience can scar the psyche deeply enough to last a lifetime. It may indeed be the effects of past anguish, still being felt, to which this card refers. This hurt might resurface and cause new problems and more missed opportunities.

This card always denotes a testing time, one of irrational or subverted trial, torment, even torture. Swept clear off your feet by sudden calamity, watching as your world disintegrates, it is sometimes difficult to keep a grip on sanity itself. Even the dreams in your troubled sleep may be full of disturbing, even diabolical, imagery. There is only one course to take; endure. Out of suffering and disillusionment, the martyr brings forth a new vision, new strength, a new beginning, and the determination that such agony will never be felt again, by anyone.

Ten of Swords

Total war, utter devastation, complete ruin, reason divorced from reality, the reign of madness, persecution, purging, chaos, violent death, abject defeat, the end.

Conflict has run riot, and now sleeps in the ruins it created. The flames of violence have engulfed the world, and flicker like snakes in a bed of ashes. What truth there ever was is re-written in the blood of the innocent. War itself is ended when there is none left alive to fight.

You may expect your hopes to be dashed. And not only yours. This disaster is rarely suffered alone; it is on a grand scale. There is little comfort in this, however, save that companionship forged in dire emergency may endure the midnight harrowing and endure into a new dawn.

There might also be some consolation to be found in the notion that the inevitable and the unexpected could soon be met with equal passion; matters can hardly get worse.

It may be that these catastrophic events are linked to involvement with a group or exclusive society. If so, then the traditional advice is to quit and go it alone.

83

Princess of Swords

This young woman applies her intellect to the pursuit of matters that are hidden, perhaps deliberately (as in espionage) or without intent, such as historical research. Being able to perceive that which underlies surface appearances makes her a skilful negotiator and ambassador. Given these talents, she particularly enjoys the opportunity to take risks based on her own judgement.

As a lover, she may take some winning, but will prove to be an honest and trustworthy partner.

Metaphorically, this card may also advise that her character traits are/should be uppermost in your own mind, or be a warning against irresponsibility, frivolity, disloyalty, and the use of merciless cunning in pursuit of unworthy goals.

Prince of Swords

This young man is quick-witted, inventive, courageous, chivalrous, impulsive, idealistic and proud. Keen to challenge injustice, he is a valiant champion of the abused. His method of attack is invariably intellectual, and his weapons are ideas. As he gains understanding and learns from experience, his opinions and the causes he espouses may change, making him appear inconsistent, but his motives remain pure.

In love, he could lack tenderness, but is nevertheless good-hearted and honest.

Metaphorically, this card might also advise that his character traits are/should be uppermost in your own mind, or be a warning against recklessness, impatience, fanaticism, and starting things you cannot (or can't be bothered to) finish.

Queen of Swords

This mature woman is self-conscious, self-reliant, and deliberate in her actions. She is perceptive, shrewd, capable, solitary and career oriented. Her acts are calculated and carefully reasoned, and she would wish that others were equally disciplined. She is also versatile, insightful, and quick to notice intricate details.

Not by nature a romantic woman, she may prove extremely unwilling to be seduced by mere protestations of love.

Metaphorically, this card might also advise that her character traits are/should be uppermost in your own mind, or be a warning against bitterness, cruelty, conceit, artifice, alienation, posturing, deviousness and overweening ambition.

King of Swords

This mature man is, at heart, a skilful judge. He uses his vast intelligence to decide issues, and craves the authority and power to put decisions to practical use. He is courageous, daring, individualistic in his interpretation of the law, and implacable when challenged. He is a champion of radical updates of ancient ideas, and delights in loosing the bonds of tradition wherever it has become anachronistic and a hindrance to progress, especially when it is an obstacle to his own ambition.

In love, he might be unemotional, even harsh, but is a stalwart protector of the family.

Metaphorically, this card may advise that his character traits are/should be uppermost in your own mind, or be a warning against tyranny, cruelty, nepotism, narrow-mindedness, obsession, selfishness and aggression.

Cups

This suit deals with our sensitivity, receptivity, imagination, and the quiet or tender moods and emotions, including romance and love. Artistic creativity (especially arising from the subconscious mind) and the appreciation of art are included in this suit, as are intuition and psychic abilities. Although these traits are often stereotyped as basically feminine, they are an essential part of all humanity. Indeed, they are often the very features that characterise us as humane as opposed to bestial.

If there is a preponderance of Cups in a spread, the reading indicates a situation that involves a good deal of self-absorption, and is fundamentally inward-looking and reflective. This introspection may, for example, be manifested by paying greater attention to friends and family. If the cards are unfavourable, it might indicate that there is a tendency to live too much in a fantasy world of make-believe.

Ace of Cups

Revelation, a vision, satori, inspiration, joy, optimism, hope, reward, nourishment, fulfilment, abundance, unlimited possibilities, liberation.

A new, more profound awareness of any situation brings additional opportunities for personal growth. This card indicates a powerful emotional bond between you and the matter in hand, which may, of course, be another person. It also suggests that the relationship is mutually beneficial and worthy of commitment and support.

The twin maternal traits of protection and nurture are strongly suggested by this card, as is motherhood. You may, therefore, receive unexpected help either in warding off some impending difficulty or in actively promoting your activities. It is a good time to enjoy freedom of expression.

This Cup is often regarded as the emblem of the Holy Grail, and the cornucopia of plenty. We are also reminded that joy is an internal experience; it may often manifest as a response to external stimuli, but unless we are open and receptive to the emotion, it cannot enter our hearts.

Two of Cups

Romantic love, friendship, trust, fellowship, union, mutual respect and admiration, exchange of ideas and gifts, harmony, sympathy.

This indicates a meeting of two people, each with much to give, and the simple pleasure they find in sharing. It represents the gentle warmth of two individuals enjoying each other's company. Even so, this attraction is tinged with the glowing possibility that affection could be fanned into passion.

This card may also indicate reconciliation. It could signify an amicable conclusion to a feud or disagreement. It might also suggest a mutually beneficial business arrangement, perhaps a contract that is fairly made between equals, especially as partners. In essence, this card suggests that two opposites are now being united.

Three of Cups

Abundance, plenty, fertility, increasing success, fruitfulness, continuing progress, enjoyment of achievement, fulfilment.

Perhaps this card marks the passing of the first real milestone of a burgeoning collaboration. Possibly it is a reunion of friends who promise to enjoy a closer relationship in the future. Maybe it is simply the feeling we get when the world seems to walk hand in hand with us as we pursue a worthy course. Whatever the particular circumstances, the cause for celebration is real and the merriment should be wholehearted and natural.

Comfort and trust are the hallmarks of this situation. With these in abundance, there is the real prospect of growth for any matter in hand. This card often indicates a birth, either literally or of some new stage in your life. If there is illness or pain, it brings healing. If there is already good cheer, it presages exuberance.

Where there is the potential for new beginnings, this card can offer the confidence to start a long journey. Be warned, though, that it is beyond the capacity of this card to forecast whether the ultimate end of such a journey is as sweet as its starting. Savour the moment by all means, but remember that everything changes.

Four of Cups
Contentment, sufficiency, luxury, rest, repose, familiarity, idleness, boredom, day-dreaming, flights of fancy.

A prolonged period during which all emotional needs are catered for. Such a spell will mean different things to different people. On the one hand, it could be a much-needed rest after a period of intense struggle and disappointment. On the other, it may appear as an almost stifling stasis, a cloying stagnation.

For most people, it can be enjoyed for its own sake, and if used wisely, could strengthen mind and body for a renewal of activity and the subsequent confrontation of new challenges. Only when its luxurious and even lethargic depth of comfort is indulged in too thirstily does this card represent a problem. Most of us could benefit from the emotional release to be gained from entertaining a little fantasy in our lives. For a few, such pleasures can become addictive, and the risks of establishing a pattern of dissipation should not be lightly ignored.

Five of Cups
Disturbance, expectations dashed, disappointment, disenchantment, depression, regret, despair, dissipation, rejection, decay.

The feelings that are stirred up here are negative in that they tend to dismantle and break down rather than support or uplift. The force of change has brought a reversal. Something of immense emotional value has been lost and there is the poignant realisation that events will never be the same again. Whether the loss was through negligence, simple chance or fate, the card does not say. However, it does indicate that the loss is only partial and not complete.

All querents need to be encouraged not to abandon themselves to dismay. Instead, they should be advised to turn aside from fruitless dwelling on dismal reflections, and seek to find solace in what yet remains of substance and worth, however meagre it may appear at this time.

The seeds within a withered and unappetising fruit still offer the miracle of fertility. It may be unpalatable at the time, but remember, to be disillusioned is to be dis-illusioned, and liberation from any blinding falsehood is ultimately to be celebrated.

Six of Cups

Joy, sustainable happiness, generosity, pleasure, well-being, calm, the discovery of affection, appreciation of simple wonders, renewal.

As if welling up from a spring and accumulating in a great pool, tender emotions are released and trickle into their exploration of a brand new world. Embracing new friendships and experiences is natural for anyone with an open-hearted approach to life. Likewise, generosity and open-handedness (with eyes equally wide open, of course) are depicted by this card.

It may be that overcoming present challenges will entail the reawakening of long-dormant talents. Reminiscences of past happiness are also indicated, especially if they help to smooth the way and ease any potential irritation by spreading the balm of peace and contentment.

Seven of Cups

Indecision, bewildering choice, lack of self-confidence, uncertainty, dalliance, lethargy, apathy.

This is no mere crossroads in your destiny: there are far more than four directions to be considered. All the opportunities and prospects in the world are arrayed for your perusal, each in its most resplendent form and inviting selection. Which to choose? How to choose? This is not the time for rational thinking; it is time to follow your heart.

People unused to feeling their way emotionally find this a particularly difficult challenge. A few may even prefer to pretend that making the choice is impossible, and will sink into self-doubt, misery, and guilt at their failings. If this is their choice, so be it!

This card merely points out the traditional attractions of wealth, prestige, power, knowledge, freedom, love and the spiritual life. Of these, of course, the occultist will assert that only the latter leads to permanent enjoyment of the fruits of the quest; all others are subject to material decay. However, many mystics affirm that all roads lead to heaven (eventually!), and that the choice is absolutely free and at the sole discretion of every individual.

Eight of Cups

Disenchantment, loss of commitment, disinterest, dissatisfaction, lack of fulfilment, counsel of despair, renunciation, relinquishment.

This card represents a moment when suddenly everything around you loses its appeal. Nothing has actually changed, except you. Where your life was once full, now it seems empty. Nothing moves you. You have become a stranger in your own house.

Perhaps you have opened your eyes a little wider than normal and realised that you have become confined. It feels as though your heart has had enough of suffering in silence and escaped, leaving you stranded and alone. It takes time for this feeling to have its full effect. This purgatory is characterised by indolence. There is profound sorrow here.

Something needs to be done to remedy the situation. Sometimes, you can simply turn your back and literally walk away. Other times, this is not such an easy option, especially where family responsibilities are concerned. Here, an inner journey is recommended; a spiritual quest to heal and revitalise the soul. In either instance, a new beginning is forecast.

Nine of Cups

Increasing joy, the gift of happiness, satisfaction guaranteed, life overflowing with pleasure, generosity of spirit, hospitality, a banquet of delight, love.

As if everything touched turns instantly to gold, there seems to be no end to the good fortune signified by this card. Whatever it is that brings happiness, this card is its courier.

Specifically, this is a fresh start, and represents the initial optimism that characterises any truly worthy venture. The power of these positive emotions is sufficient to turn water into wine, autumn leaves into faery treasure, and ideas into actions. This is a card of transmutation, the alchemy of love.

Ten of Cups
Heartfelt satisfaction, arrival at (or return to) one's home, rapture, ecstasy, complete contentment, satiety.

All the affairs of the heart are settled and harmonious. There is a peaceful and secure environment, especially with respect to one's friends and family. Everything you could hope for is either achieved or attainable now. There is nothing more you need in order to feel emotionally fulfilled. Even the thrilling excitement of the most important quest you can imagine is included in this complex card of conclusive arrival and intimate belonging.

This is the card of perfect success. It can also mark, for example, the discovery (or vision) of the spiritual essence within physical matter.

Once experienced, there is a part of its power that can never be taken away (as in any rite of passage), but it is wise to cherish the moment, for everything under the sun is subject to change.

Princess of Cups
This young woman is calm and serene, gentle, kind and voluptuous. She is also quiet, studious, sensitive, sentimental, even poetic, and will give excellent advice if called upon.

She is deeply conscious of the changing tides that shape the world. She is adaptable and receptive to new ideas, yet can intuitively distinguish a mere superficial notion from a solid, practical plan. This faculty enables her to hold a position of great power in the world, for she can eliminate the frivolous and nurture the worthy.

Because of her rich inner life, she can easily tolerate levels of monotony and boredom in her career that few others could endure for long. However, if her nature is taken for granted or abused, her sense of loyalty will quickly evaporate and she may suddenly disappear.

In love, she is very sensitive towards her lover's needs and desires.

Metaphorically, this card may also advise that her character traits are/should be uppermost in your own mind, or be a warning against scheming, deception, resentment, indolence and insecurity.

Prince of Cups

This young man is an enthusiastic seeker, rarely able to remain in one situation for long, and is always eager to find and pursue new opportunities and ideas. His mind is as bright and agile as quicksilver, and seeks to be loyal to any course laid before him. However, he will always follow his own heart first and foremost, so even if it causes him embarrassment, he may need to change his allegiance fairly frequently.

Partly because of his lust for new experiences and environments, he is often seen as a mysterious stranger. His romantic image is fostered by a deep fascination with distant and unknown places, haunting ideas and occult powers.

In affairs of the heart, he tends towards the romantic, and might even idealise love.

Metaphorically, this card may also advise that his character traits are/should be uppermost in your own mind, or be a warning against lack of concentration, inability to face facts, being easily misled, unreliability, trickery, lack of commitment and false promises.

Queen of Cups

This mature woman is graceful, bounteous, sensitive to the needs of others, a superlative ambassador, wise, artistic, imaginative, meditative and loving. She is also essentially unfathomable, and has a profound inner communion with the unconscious, giving her apparently psychic abilities.

Her attention is never directed on actions, but always on the causes and results of those actions. She follows only that course laid down by the movements of her own heart. She cannot be misled, tricked or hypnotised.

91

She is a considerate lover, with an alluring manner that many find irresistible. She may appear to be all things to all men.

Metaphorically, this card might also advise that her character traits are/should be uppermost in your own mind, or be a warning against slander, betrayal of confidences, subjectivity, pretence, and living in a dream world.

King of Cups

This mature man is, despite the power of his own authority, unable to rest upon his laurels. He is actively seeking the fulfilment of his inner vision. He is idealistic and charismatic, intensely heroic yet vulnerably human. He is consistent in his continually renewed effort to bring out the best in humanity. To this end, he is himself pure of heart and fired with enthusiasm.

The goal of his quest is, unfortunately, beyond the imagination of many people (who would call it utopian or idealistic), and consider him cool and aloof from the problems of everyday folk. He may, however, be respected and cherished as a noble and high-minded eccentric.

He is cultured, an independent thinker, a patron of the arts and sciences, and a keen upholder of the right of law against the forces of anarchy.

In love, he could be uneasy with his own emotions, have a low libido, and dislike showing affection openly.

Metaphorically, this card may also advise that his character traits are/should be uppermost in your own mind, or be a warning against impossible dreams, profligate squandering of resources, irresponsibility, injustice, abuse of social status, conceit, melancholia and self-abuse.

Wands

This suit represents will power – pure and simple. This may be visualised as a magic wand. You hold one end of the wand in your hand (this is the idea that you wish to be fulfilled); the shaft is your will power. At the other tip of the wand is the object of your desire. Hey presto! You project yourself along the line of your will, though it may actually take days, even years, and you achieve your end.

Will power can be intensely passionate or quietly smouldering. Whichever, it vivifies and directs our lives, and sustains us through times of adversity. Enthusiasm, excitement, the surge of creative inspiration, and the burning force of ambition are all represented by this suit.

A preponderance of Wands indicates a period or situation involving a crescendo of emotional energy, during which you will need to sustain a high level of activity just to keep abreast of events. If most cards are unfavourable, you are advised to anticipate having a major battle on your hands.

Ace of Wands

Energy, will, passion, aspiration, ambition, desire, excitement, enthusiasm, activity, motivation, innovation.

This Ace has the power of pure creativity at its fingertips. As free and fierce as fire, actions now speak much louder than words. It may, indeed, be necessary now to fight fire with fire. This is to say that it might be advisable to meet every force that acts against you with an equal and opposite force.

This card could also have something of the nature of the battering ram about it; opening up new possibilities, barging into new territory, and generally overcoming resistance.

It strongly signifies new beginnings, new enterprises, inspiration, invention and original ideas.

Two of Wands

Partnership, mutual support, co-operation, joint endeavour, strength in numbers, equitable division of the rewards of success.

By helping each other in an organised and fair system, individuals can prosper more readily than if they squander resources in competition and strife.

Despite the prospect of material achievements, this arrangement can bring a humbling awareness of being but a cog on a wheel. This sense of having command of your particular part of the mechanism of government, while simultaneously being under the direct control of others higher in the hierarchy, gives some people a welcome feeling of security. To others it is anathema, as it seems to deprive them of their much-valued independence of action. Such people need to appreciate the importance of the grand scheme of which they are a vital part.

The key to progressing to higher levels within this system is to understand and deal fairly with both of those opposing points of view. This card indicates that there is an immediate prospect of this career ascendancy. Advantage is, however, traditionally said to be dependent on making a crucial decision without delay.

Three of Wands

Momentum, escape velocity, energy unleashed, a chain reaction, force out of control, consuming passion.

What was set in motion is now proceeding. It is out of your hands. For better or for worse, your enterprise is up and running on its own two feet! Whether it will prosper depends largely, of course, on how well the project was initiated.

This is a testing time, and there is little to be done now except to watch and see how it fares. However, there are some grounds for confidence as this card carries a traditional meaning of dreams coming true, and the establishment of a successful reputation.

This card carries an additional meaning: the sudden and irrevocable publication of a powerful secret. Again, the consequences must be faced with steady nerves as the affair runs its course.

Four of Wands

A power base, headquarters, command centre, community spirit, established strength.

Diverse matters have been integrated into a single, vigorous entity. This coming together represents a culmination or completion of the essential first phase of a major project. The next stage is for the newly formed group or collaboration to start actually doing whatever it was set up to achieve. Note that this card alone cannot forecast the ultimate success or otherwise of the venture, although it does indicate a successful beginning. It certainly suggests there is currently cause for celebration in that all the key elements have been assembled and are now in place, ready for use.

Although this card is often taken to indicate a firm foundation to a successful career (e.g. the gaining of appropriate qualifications), it can also entertain specific meanings as diverse as buying a stamp album, a tool set, or packing your cases for a holiday.

Five of Wands

Clash of wills, violent disagreement, conflict, strife, struggle, vigorous opposition, unrestrained competition, impassioned argument.

An inescapable confrontation is signified. This may be an instance of an unstoppable force meeting an immovable object, or simply the head-on meeting of proponents of opposite points of view. Whichever, this card indicates that the flash point has been reached, and passions kindled into fierce flames of hostility.

You need to ask yourself this question: is the bone of contention really worth fighting for?

It is always possible that heated negotiations can take the place of a real and damaging contest of strength. Much here depends upon the character of the protagonists. The card may be seen as a warning that, if taken to heart, can enable damage-limitation measures to be implemented. On the other hand, it could be viewed as a signal that the time is right to mount a decisive strike against the opposition.

Six of Wands

Accomplishment, success, victory, triumph, the crowning moment, attainment, mastery.

Victory can be a bitter-sweet experience, where the pain and loss from the battle itself are balanced with the pleasure and relief of winning the field. Whether the victory is hollow or richly rewarding, this card is unequivocal in its estimation that the fighting is certainly over and done with, and the day is truly won. It signals recognition and honours from your peers, and the achievement of an elevated status.

This card carries the parallel meanings of the arrival of good news, liberation from anxiety, and the fulfilment of hope.

Seven of Wands

Valour, fortitude, courage, bravery, gallantry, self-confidence, independence, virility.

Despite the prospect of combating overwhelming odds, unless you are true to yourself and stand up for what you believe in now, worse misfortune will befall. If you capitulate without putting up a fight, greater damage will be done than would be sustained by engaging in and even losing the battle itself.

Traditionally, this card offers the assurance that not only is the struggle worthy, but also (notwithstanding appearances) distinctly winnable. This card indicates that skill, resilience, tenacity and determination will all be needed, but the effort rewarded with success. The struggle is basically an heroic one, where a single individual is all that stands in the path of disorder, confusion and degeneracy.

Eight of Wands

Prompt action, swift and effective movement, decisive response, energetic investigation, versatile and holistic activity.

Leaving no stone unturned, you must attend simultaneously to a great many matters. It is time to mobilise all the forces at your command. There is an equilibrium of danger and opportunity, and only quick thinking and vigorous action can repel the one and embrace the other. Even the merest details must be settled before success is assured.

Haste is the decisive element here with speed and sure-footedness. This is the time to seize the initiative, send urgent messages, make important journeys, and initiate bold new designs. This card shows us that excitement and activity are now the heralds of success.

Nine of Wands

Strength, inner power, self-confidence, certitude, conviction, belief, faith, resolve, steadfastness, stability.

Rightly or wrongly, a stance and a course of action are determined and nothing will alter them. There is a powerful sense of resolution and self-assurance, which will withstand any argument and tolerate no opposition. This card depicts a situation where even the mere idea of backing down is utterly unthinkable.

There may be many challenges and obstacles to overcome, but all will be faced steadfastly and with fortitude. There might be delays in achieving personal goals, but the way forward is through single-mindedness and perseverance. This card portrays a situation where the physical body is the willing and able tool of the mind, and will power is the governing force.

Ten of Wands

Oppression, stifling pressure, abuse of power, fanaticism, mania, rampant egotism, unrestrained animal passions, stress overload.

It may be that you are simply trying to do too many things all at the same time. You must ask yourself whether you are stretching yourself too thinly. If so, you will end up achieving nothing worth enjoying, especially as your health is likely to suffer from the stress.

When the will of a person or an institution becomes over-bearing, its influence is a burden that can only be carried with pain and resentment. The weak labour endlessly under the will of the strong. The strong, through their very strength and success, have become corrupt and depraved, and lord it over their fellows and despoil their own environment. The outlook is bleak, but not beyond remedy. Counselling is probably advisable.

Princess of Wands

This young woman is not only very energetic, but also strongly spontaneous. She has a vibrant personality with a smouldering passion for life. She is ambitious, effective and hard-working in her chosen career, delighting in challenges. She may also be outspoken and forthright, confident of her abilities and have complete self-assurance. That she is also impulsive may give rise to a characteristic of being accident-prone. Indeed, sudden, irrational outbursts of passion (of love or hate, and in equal measure) are another hallmark of her temperament.

She brings a refreshing innocence and simple joy to romance.

Metaphorically, this card may also advise that her character traits are/should be uppermost in your own mind, or be a warning against being brash, a gossip, scandal-mongering, bragging, bearing false witness, blind to your own failings, and showing contempt for other people's feelings.

Prince of Wands

This young man is ardent, adventurous, and impulsive in all his dealings. He is exceptionally quick-witted, and also very vigorous in promoting his ideas. Equally, he is vehement in the defence of his friends and espoused causes. Essentially, though, he is fun-loving and prefers to be foot-loose and fancy-free.

The break-neck speed at which he lives his life leaves most people simply standing and staring. His capacity for work is prodigious, and his energies are dispensed with an open hand. However, as soon as he settles down in one position, his attention is caught by something completely different, and in an instant he is up and away. This characteristic often gives him an air of wildness, even of danger, and makes him socially very engaging. This card is sometimes interpreted as indicating that an unpremeditated or speedy journey is advised.

In love, he is exceptionally generous, and is always an exciting lover.

Metaphorically, this card may also advise that his character traits are/should be uppermost in your own mind, or be a warning against pride, irresponsibility, caprice, disloyalty, recklessness, discord and intolerance.

Queen of Wands

This mature woman is kind, generous, friendly, sympathetic and loving. She is also a vigorous proponent of her own opinions and beliefs. She will instinctively search carefully for the good in any proposition before undertaking to endorse, promote, embrace or instigate any positive action.

She is attentive and adaptable, but once motivated is dedicated, unswerving and determined. In fact, her determination to succeed in all her endeavours is matched only by her capability to achieve those goals. Sheer persistence is the key she uses to get through life with an air of calm authority.

In matters of love, she is sympathetic, passionate and independent.

Metaphorically, this card may also advise that her character traits are/should be uppermost in your own mind, or be a warning against impatience, fits of temper, exacting vengeance to the point of cruelty, self-righteousness and vanity.

King of Wands

This mature man is a passionate believer in his own capabilities and rights. He is virile, confident, responsible, accomplished, optimistic, generous and courageous. He is zealously dedicated to freedom of expression, unrestricted movement, new discoveries, and the evolutionary necessity of continual innovation and experimentation.

The ideas he holds are fervently cherished. They are rarely logical, although his judgements are usually sound, and his motives are unquestionably honourable. His decisions are usually creative, based on personal experience rather than any established code or convention. He is possessed of great personal magnetism, which attracts many companions who are content to bask in the glory of his charisma.

In love, he is receptive, understanding, witty and affectionate.

Metaphorically, this card may also advise that his character traits are/should be uppermost in your own mind, or be a warning against tyranny, fanaticism, prejudice, undue severity and impetuosity.

5

The Major Arcana

The Fool

A remarkable adventure is either just beginning or is taking an altogether unprecedented turn.

Despite its name, this card rarely represents foolishness, although it does frequently indicate actions that are utterly spontaneous and unpremeditated. Whether the course of events will be advantageous depends upon other influences as revealed by associated cards in a spread. However, tradition stresses the existence of a factor, powerful but at present unknown, which is both guiding and protecting the Fool. This is often symbolised pictorially by an animal that is alerting the Fool to imminent danger. The Tarot reader must share the burden of this creature and warn the querent that unless he or she spends a little less time worrying about the future or the past, the present will be jeopardised. If you are the querent, take pains to discover who or what is trying to alert you.

Originality and eccentricity are hallmarks of any situation indicated by this card. It can denote the profound influence of a stranger, and also that some form of salvation will come from a completely unexpected source.

This card symbolises a time of actively following intuition, but do not gamble more than you can afford to lose. Although it can signify the start of a spiritual quest, it usually indicates more mundane matters, such as simply enjoying a break from humdrum routine. This could be anything from taking an extended lunch break in order to explore some unfamiliar shops, to an adventure holiday in an exotic wilderness.

Reversed, the Fool issues a warning that circumstances may suddenly cause you to lose control of a situation, and specifically advises making adequate contingency plans. It is time to pay close attention to nagging details otherwise those long-term hopes you are dreaming of will be dashed, with no one to blame but yourself.

The Magician

A period of calm control is indicated, in which all the important elements will fall naturally into place.

It is vital now to maintain a firm grasp (or a sharp eye, at least) on the details of a situation. The key to success is concentration. Take care to neglect nothing.

An opportunity is ripe for the right person to take control of the helm. It may be time to demonstrate (or discover) self-confidence and your ability to lead from the front. Especially in supporting those causes for which you feel most deeply, this is the time to do your best to help. Be bold, even daring, and put yourself forward as a candidate. This card insists that if you do not try as hard as you can right now, you will inevitably fail – big time.

Determination, diplomacy, adaptability, energy, initiative and commitment are the characteristics that will be most helpful. It may be that these qualities are possessed by someone who will unexpectedly show you a way out of present troubles, as if by magic.

Reversed, this card offers a warning: let one thing slip your mind and an entire enterprise could crumble around your feet. It can also indicate a situation, not necessarily of your making, characterised by the abuse of power, which turns hope of improvement into crushing despair.

The High Priestess

The solution to a problem can only be found by stepping back from confrontation, and seeing the whole situation in a broader context.

The High Priestess is the keeper of the mysteries. She does not withhold the truth from anyone, but has learned that spiritual truths (and many others beside) become unintelligible when they are spoken aloud. She teaches us how to listen to the eloquent silence within our own souls, the fount of inner power.

This card proposes a period of withdrawing, of reflection, meditation and peace. Dreams and other means of assessing the subconscious for clues (including divination) are particularly recommended.

Allowing any artistic or poetic impulses full rein is one such method, irrespective of how talented you think you are. The results can be both surprising and enlightening. This card is often the harbinger of enlightening inspiration.

It is now possible to learn one of life's vital lessons: all the information is at your fingertips. It is only necessary to review the evidence in order to make the discovery. You have the knowledge already; only a deeper understanding is needed to bring a difficult or confused situation into harmony and fruitfulness. This may be experienced as a gentle awakening or a sudden revelation. Whichever, it is an initiation into a larger universe.

It may be that there is someone working behind the scenes who would be a great ally in troublesome times. This help could be nothing more than a wise word at the right time, but such tiny events can change the entire course of history.

Reversed, anticipate stinging slander and malicious gossip. There may be no substance in the rumours, but they still have the power to wound. It might be that a dignified silence is the only defence, that and the truth, however painful it feels at the moment.

The Empress
Time spent in looking after the home and ensuring that loved ones are well taken care of will be amply rewarded.

Comfort, security, sensuality, and taking pleasure in the simple things in life are all indicated by this card. It also advises getting in touch with the natural cycle of the seasons, learning to see your life in the grander perspective of nature as a whole, and discovering your own feelings, yearnings and needs.

It suggests the artistic vision, and the perception of beauty in people, places and things. This can amount to an almost spiritual revelation of wonderment at the mere fact of existence.

Sympathy, honesty, persuasion by seduction, fertility, nurture and maternal care are all hallmarks of this card.

The fact that the Empress is, traditionally, pregnant, may account for this card's association with ventures and enterprises coming into fruition. It therefore indicates a time to enjoy garnering the results of your labour. A period of prosperity, even plenty, is suggested. Certainly a situation of emotional well-being is depicted.

Reversed, it suggests the accumulation and flaunting of items of opulence. It indicates material acquisitions gained by rapacious exploitation, and at the expense of incalculable suffering.

The Emperor
In the present situation, it is advisable to negotiate if you wish, and delegate if you must, but do not desert your post for an instant.

The Emperor suggests that it is imperative to maintain calm now, even when at the centre of a whirlwind. The Emperor's sense of composed control, of personal authority, carries such conviction that it can dominate a situation to the extent that opposition disperses, its threatened challenge amounting to nothing more than foolish posturing.

The ability to direct the actions of other people, to use the chain of command, even to pull rank where necessary, are all hallmarks of established power. If you are to rise above a present difficulty, these are the characteristics that you must bring to bear on the situation. Similarly, discipline, self-control, courage and willpower are all essential qualities that will be called upon before this matter is satisfactorily finished.

Under a benign government, a period of stability will bring prosperity, during which many worthy projects can grow and flourish. The Emperor may indicate such a situation, or even signify the influence of a powerful friend.

Reversed meanings indicate brutality and the triumph of mere strength over virtue.

The High Priest
Resurgence out of self-absorption, and renewed interest in the world, bring undreamed-of opportunities within your reach.

The forging or renewal of personal relationships (over a broad spectrum) affords not only an increasing engagement in social events, but also an enlargement of your influence over local events. Participation is the key to unlocking the potential of the present situation. Be prepared to give generously and without obligation or thought of reward, and also to receive with humility and joy.

It may be that your beliefs (especially of a religious nature) are challenged. Applying traditional values to contemporary situations is not always easy, and advice from a respected authority or cultural leader may be helpful now in forming an opinion on a complex moral dilemma.

Rejuvenation and a sense of awakening are hallmarks of this card. Honesty, integrity, practicality, simplicity, transparency of motive and social responsibility are key characteristics to be brought to the fore.

Reversed meanings include blind superstition, deception, trickery, false promises and hypocrisy.

The Lovers

The excitement of mutual affection grows as a relationship becomes closer and more intense.

Passion, ecstasy, and the rapture of intimate exploration are indicated by this card but, to be fair, the interpretation is rarely so literal. Unfortunate, perhaps, but true. Often, the Lovers simply suggest that your personal relationship/s are going to feature heavily in your life. The prognosis for the health and well-being of these relationships is certainly good, but not necessarily thrilling and lusty! Sorry.

Devotion, constancy, harmony, unity, honesty and self-discovery are essential ingredients of the situation. Other characteristics include action independent of established authority, emotional release, opening-up, flash of insight, developing new interests, going to new places, and meeting new people.

There is also the possibility of facing a great challenge, but you will not do so alone. In this case, the card advises that you seek to unite opposing factions in order to bring peace. It further suggests that just as a butterfly can only develop following the dissolution of its caterpillar phase, we only grow into a new and more highly evolved condition by virtue of love's power of transmutation.

Reversed, the Lovers indicate either irritating misunderstandings or a cooling of affection.

The Chariot

Major changes are underway: unexpected twists and turns in events are coming thick and fast, and you are being swept along at breakneck speed.

A powerful force is flowing through your life. If you can take the reins, exercise control, and determine the direction in which you are travelling, you will be assured of a speedy and successful conclusion of a vitally important matter.

This card may also indicate a physical relocation. Usually, this would be more permanent than a mere holiday. If a trip is already planned, this card indicates that the journey may prove far more eventful and significant than previously thought.

The key to negotiating these changing times is concentration. You need to keep your destination and goal firmly fixed in your mind. While it is essential to make minor course adjustments in order to avoid the obstacles that may yet lie in your path, your mind needs to be fixed on the long-term objective and not allow itself to be distracted. Commitment to an ultimate goal may be tested here. The personality, the vehicle of the spirit, might also be exposed to considerable stress, revealing chinks and cracks in your psychic armour.

Reversed. Especially if associated cards are gloomy, this card indicates you are the victim of forces beyond your control. Like a beggar in a gale, there is little to do but sit tight and wait for the storm to pass. Otherwise, it may suggest that you are being insensitive to the vulnerability of those affected by your own haughty actions.

Justice

Under scrutiny from discriminating judges, that which is faulty is dispensed with, while that which is worthy is exalted.

An investigation is underway which will provide a platform both for the exposure of lies and the discovery of truth. As none of us is exemplary all the time, admitting to certain secrets unearthed during this process may be an uncomfortable experience. If you are involved in adjudicating this procedure, it is essential to be scrupulously fair and unbiased, and to weigh the evidence and arguments with equal consideration.

This may literally involve the legal profession, and even amount to a court case. More often, it suggests a minor inquiry or inspection, at work for example, or an academic examination. It might indicate business negotiations and/or the reaching of an important agreement. However, its meaning could also be found in a bit of soul-searching during a sleepless night.

An impartial examination of personal traits aims to identify useful and redundant factors, and to treat them appropriately. Its aim is not so much to punish negative or reward positive elements, but to maintain the balance and potential for future growth of the individual within a healthy society.

The outcome of any such inquisition needs to be taken very seriously. If you are found to have broken some written law or code of behaviour, along with culpability for the lapse, you need to accept the responsibility of changing your ways.

It may also represent the awakening of conscience, where some past wrongdoing returns to haunt you, prompting you to undertake a voluntary act of specific recompense or general repentance.

Reversed, the case against you is formidable. In order to save yourself, you will need to muster a very carefully constructed and detailed defence.

The Hermit

Learning to trust ourselves, we seek solitude so we might better hear the quiet inner voice that is so easily drowned in the crowded hubbub of day-to-day life.

The Hermit moves through the world yet is not moved by it. Instead, his attention is wholeheartedly devoted to his quest for something more meaningful and fulfilling than surface appearances. He is alive to the prospect of happiness, plenty and love, but mourns their impermanence. He is seeking to understand the causes of all the woes of the world in order to find and promote their cure. At last, questioning the very sense of the questions he has set out to answer, as if lost in the darkest night, he is freed from dogma, preconceptions and deceit. There is an element of rebirth inherent in this card.

Whether wounded by love or alienated by intolerance, driven by fear or inspired by high ideals, we all sooner or later consciously embark upon a voyage of self-discovery. For many people, this is something that happens when your life nose-dives into a world of hurt. That process can be very painful indeed. This card offers the option of awakening to the benefits that self-knowledge can bring (not least of which are increased self-confidence and wisdom), before fortune forces your hand. It strongly advocates spending some time and energy on the enterprise, which might, after all, be the best investment you ever make.

At a mundane level, this card suggests that rather than continuing with an established strategy, it is wise to reconsider your proposed actions. It advises you should conscientiously check that your plans are appropriate and adequately robust before entrusting your fortunes to them.

Reversed, it indicates self-delusion, loneliness, confusion, ignorance, futility, lack of self-discipline and sorrow.

The Wheel of Fortune
That which has been ascendant will slip into decline, and that which was abased will be exalted.

Change is afoot! An environment of confusion, almost chaotic but not quite, is sweeping away the old, and establishing a new order. At such a time, everyone must look to their own interests lest they be dragged down by a sinking ship. It is a time when innovation can thrive on a wealth of opportunities that are simply there for the taking. But so swiftly can the fluctuations of fortune swing from boom to bust, and from profit to loss, that there is little security in investing right now.

This is, perhaps, a good time to be a generalist, to have your assets in a broad spectrum of interests, and to play safe and risk nothing. On the other hand, you might be poised on the brink of the time of your life and all you have to do is plunge in.

It is essential now to have your wits about you and try to maintain your sense of balance (and humour!) as the rug is whisked firmly out from under your feet. At very least, a new cycle of life is starting, for better or for worse. It is time to reap what has been sown.

Reversed, it indicates that matters are out of control. You can expect a change for the worse involving the deterioration in an important enterprise, and disintegration and loss. The best that can be hoped for is that you learn from your mistakes.

Strength
Animal passions and the fierce energy they can bring to bear on any situation need to be integrated into a creative lifestyle.

It may be that raw emotions have been running away with you, and that you need to exercise an increased measure of self-control in order to prevent yourself from falling into disrepute. Perhaps you need to relax too strenuous a discipline (tantamount to repression), and ought to allow your feelings the release of expression by channelling them in a socially acceptable direction. Whichever, this card reminds you that you are always intimately involved in the dance of life.

A key message is that you should dare to enjoy your individuality just as you ought to encourage other people to feel free to enjoy theirs. Do not be ashamed of your human nature. Rather, work with it, and seek to harmonise yourself with your environment. Some people regard this as the most powerfully affirmative card in the pack, suggesting that who you are is more significant than what you do.

Traditionally, this card recommends that gentleness and loving kindness are the best ways now to defeat a powerful adversary. A more modern approach might be to suggest that vigour and vitality in pursuit of your own interests will distance you from the clutches of an enemy who relies on dragging you down to their own level of grappling confrontation.

Reversed meanings include brutality, self-abuse, mania, alienation, and all forms of anti-social behaviour.

The Hanged Man
We all have to suffer the consequences of our actions and, naturally, sometimes the suffering is worse than others; be prepared now for the worst!

This card indicates that our fate has been taken out of our hands. Decisions are being taken for us rather than by us. It advises that it is now wiser to surrender than to fight. We may not find it easy to bow to authority, of whatever sort, but this card suggests that the very act of choosing to submit is actually a positive affirmation of self-determination. This may seem a mere crumb of cold comfort, but it serves to remind you that all is not lost.

Indeed, this card stresses the value of sacrifice. It emphasises the good sense of giving up voluntarily something that is of little worth (or even harmful, such as a bad habit), so that something better can take its place.

Sometimes, we are called upon to perform an act of self-sacrifice, where the beneficiary is somebody else. Such actions are traditionally held to attract rewards of a spiritual nature. The appearance of this card in a spread may suggest that the time has come to reject personal satisfaction and pleasure, intently pursuing instead the well-being of your loved ones and peers.

Certainly, this card indicates that something of importance is being lost, but not everything. It also hints that although you might be tested to the limit of your endurance, you will gain much in the end. It is vital to muster the courage to persevere in your devotion to long-term aspirations. It is time to remember the motives that brought you to this pass, and to reconsider their value.

Reversed, this card warns you against rash promises and commitments to impractical schemes. Past misdemeanours may return to haunt you, and compensation could be punitive. Heavy losses are to be anticipated. There is little hope of salvaging anything worthwhile.

Death
The conclusion of a project, enterprise, or ambition is at hand: it may be untimely, even sudden and utterly unexpected, but is unquestionably finished.

This card represents a challenge that is difficult but not impossible to overcome. Ironically, the Tarot reader is also likewise made to struggle to find an interpretation beyond its literal meaning – the death of the querent! Indeed, it indicates that only by overcoming the dire obstacles that currently lie in your path can gains be made. Those gains are, incidentally, usually touted to be very significant and worthwhile indeed. Some authorities actually rejoice in this most morbid card, hailing it as the herald of the querent's entry into a new and exciting realm.

Whatever may come next, this card resolutely focuses on the forces that are causing the disintegration of your present lifestyle. Any optimism there had been for future or continued success is now confronted with the stark reality of failure or, at least, the complete lack of opportunity for further growth.

It marks the end of an important phase. Separation and estrangement may also feature in this major yet somehow inevitable change of circumstances. There could be the severing of a relationship dear to your heart. Whenever something is cut down in its prime, extreme sadness and even pangs of grief are felt by all who mourn its passing.

Reversed meanings include symptoms such as depression, morbidity, and mental breakdown, resulting from a serious loss, especially one that would have been better borne had it been arranged voluntarily and with humility.

Temperance

Like the confluence of two rivers, things are unsettled (even chaotic) while two separate identities merge and fuse into one powerful entity.

It is time to mingle. An increase in social activities can engender an invaluable cross-fertilisation of ideas. New opportunities are available now, both in relationships and business. However, to take full advantage of these prospects will demand subtle and skilful manipulation of events. It is prudent now to avoid extremes, and instead, cleave to the middle path.

Personal strength and the foundations of a healthy career can now be found in the mixing of raw elements into a new combination. This card also promotes any art or science that is involved with the fusion of ideas or chemicals into novel forms and designs. Using diverse ingredients and following a recipe to produce a culinary delight is an image replete with suggestive metaphors. This card denotes a melting-pot.

Although it urges you to retain a sense of equilibrium while everything around is in a state of flux, it is a mistake to view this card as indicating passivity. It suggests that dynamic participation is now essential in order for you to find your future happiness. Prepare to be moved, perhaps to tears. But rest assured that, traditionally at least, these would be tears of joy.

Reversed, this card indicates that changes are bringing distress, particularly because you are floundering in a swiftly moving current with little or no control over your course. It is essential to sustain or develop a clear idea of personal goals.

The Devil

The nature of things hidden is suddenly transparent; the veil of lies and the veneer of deceit are stripped away, and things can be seen for what they are.

111

In many instances, that which stands suddenly revealed produces a nasty shock. It may be that your trust has been badly misplaced, and your good faith wickedly abused. There might have been cruelty, lust and greed lurking unsuspected at the heart of an enterprise of which you were proud to be a part. Perhaps your own motives have been starkly shown to be less worthy than you believed.

On the other hand, if you were already aware that the world is still crying out for a hero to right wrongs and combat evil, this is your chance to audition for the part. But do not forget that human nature is as easily perverted by the lack of opportunities for doing good as it is tempted by selfish pleasures. The freedom to choose your own way in the world is a guiding light in this murky realm. It is also necessary to overcome fear in order to make progress.

At another level of interpretation, this card embodies the raw passion for life that burns within all living creatures; it is the will to live. As such, combating this force is fraught with paradox. Indeed, the fight is only possible in terms of sophistication: channelling primordial urges into evolutionary behaviour.

Reversed, blind impulses are usurping reason and rational behaviour. Trickery and subterfuge have caught you in a web of intrigue, from which it will not be easy to escape.

The Tower of Destruction
Things appear to be collapsing around you, literally falling apart, and threaten to hurl you into oblivion along with them.

This card denotes the violent end of a project, sometimes even of life's work, occasionally, too, of a life. All that had been carefully constructed in a balanced and orderly fashion has been cast down by a moment of disaster.

It may be that this sweeping destruction clears the ground for subsequent regeneration. Such a gloss is often put upon this card in an effort to reduce its devastating emotional impact. Perhaps a better way to put it into perspective is to realise that, often unwittingly, we become prisoners in a situation. Perhaps through no fault of our own, we are stuck in a rut of routine, frozen in inflexible attitudes and dogmatic beliefs, or captivated by an illusory promise. This card indicates release from all these prisons. It brings rescue from bondage, and freedom from false convictions and beliefs.

The hallmarks of this card are catastrophe and breakdown, but its effects are liberation and enlightenment.

Reversed, it indicates the wanton destruction of cherished and worthy works, whose rebuilding will take much time and energy.

The Star
Although distant and perhaps correspondingly difficult to reach, the attraction of a single goal or ambition is strong and inspires feats of endurance and valour.

Although there might be no realistic hope of achieving your aim at the present time, there is much you can do to make preparations. You could spend this period busily making yourself fit for the journey towards your dreams, or choose simply to rest while yet you may. Whichever, do not lose sight of the object of your aspiration, or else you might become disoriented and lost. Your deepest wishes are your guide through a testing time. Remain true to them, and they will shine like a beacon leading you forward.

It is essential now to embrace humility and adopt a conscientious approach. There may be wealth of importance in the merest detail. A wonderful opportunity might be missed if a spark of true genius is not recognised. Be scrupulous in all you elect to perform. The hallmarks of this card are inspiration and beauty.

Reversed, this card indicates false hopes, self-doubt, misplaced trust and fundamental mistakes that will eventually wreck your ambitions, and the investment of your energy in an unprofitable enterprise.

The Moon
Nothing now is quite what it seems. If by any bizarre trick of perspective anything does seem normal, it will not remain so for long.

This card indicates a time of great uncertainty. It is difficult to trust anything at all at the moment. Hidden meanings to cryptic messages have yet to be revealed, whilst devious machinations move silently just below the surface of apparently innocuous events. Beware!

Although there is the potential for taking great strides forward that bring you over the crest of an horizon to view a breathtaking panorama of opportunity beyond, remember that there is also the potential for falling from perilous mountain passes.

113

The idea of a journey is inherent in this card. Its territory is unfamiliar and there are certainly obstacles to be overcome. There is also an explicit warning not to fall prey to the glamour of a mirage or phantom. You are, in fact, in the midst of an adventure full of mystery and marvels. By all means enjoy it, but do not try to build a permanent home on its shifting sands.

The key to this card is imagination. Artistic creativity is particularly well favoured, and your dreams may hold special meanings that careful research can decipher. The symbolism of occult imagery may become transparent, and psychic development is, traditionally, assured. The way your own mental apparatus colours and/or distorts your perceptions of the world can make all the difference to the safe enjoyment of life. This is a good time to experiment with trying to look at life with a broader focus, and for seeing another person's point of view.

Reversed, there is a problem with the way you see the world. You have a distorted image of someone or something (or simply an obstructive mood, for instance), which will instigate a painful loss.

The Sun
Safety and joy accompany you, making every occasion for social or commercial activity both a pleasure and profitable.

It is easy to see how things stand. Indeed, it is crystal clear now how you must make your way through the present situation in order to reach your goal. So broad are your options, in fact, that there is ample time actively to enjoy your passage through this rejuvenating period. This card may literally indicate a holiday, or at least a welcome respite from any drudgery or anxiety.

This is also a good time for opening your heart and sharing dreams with a trusted friend. Generosity of spirit and an open-handed attitude to life are strongly recommended. You may also find yourself unexpectedly on the receiving end of another's munificence.

Enthusiasm and freedom of expression are the characteristics of this card. Its hallmark is honesty.

Reversed, this card indicates over-optimism, misjudgement, arrogance, pride, excessive confidence in your own abilities, and egotism.

Judgement
There is a powerful sense of awakening. It is as if the dawn of a new age is about to transfigure you in its new light.

A new and exciting phase of activity is beginning. The opportunities that open up before you now are your reward for success in an earlier phase of activity. Past achievement has resulted in your present fortunate position: you are ready to enjoy the fruits of your labours. Perhaps you may start to build a new ambition for yourself, but for now it is enough to recognise the sense of history as one stage of your life is firmly closed, and another is just beginning.

The hallmark of this card is an acceptance (even an embracing) of the new order, with a sense of awe and wonder. Indeed, it may be that this card indicates the sudden realisation of latent talents in yourself (especially creative or artistic) or hidden potential in your lifestyle. It could, therefore, herald a sort of rebirth, or transformation.

Reversed, the awakening is not harmonious, but rather rude, shameful, and distinctly unpleasant. It might be that you need to be dragged, kicking and screaming, into the light of the new day. It can also indicate wasted opportunities.

The World
The will to participate in every aspect of life, coupled with the infinite possibilities it offers, produces a most satisfactory lifestyle!

This card denotes the successful culmination of a journey or enterprise. The achievement of your goals and ambitions enables you to indulge in living your dream come true. Moreover, there is such harmony in your situation that the good fortune marking this particular high point in your life is likely to have a lasting effect on your future well-being.

The victor's wreath is your hallmark of attainment. Although resting on your laurels is traditionally inadvisable, their noble leaves can certainly help to feather your nest for a considerable time to come.

This card specifically represents the ultimate synthesis of disparate elements. Diverse factors have been united into a balanced order that will continually and liberally produce benefits.

Reversed, this card indicates the attainment of only a hollow victory. Something sours what should be a celebration, and the fruit of your labour is bitter.

6
Tarot Mysteries

Apart from its use as an oracle, the pictures that form the Tarot (especially the Major Arcana) are regarded as symbols of sublime mysteries. Tarot scholars throughout the ages have likened them to keys that can open the student's mind to spiritual illumination. By its very nature, the subject matter in this chapter is relatively advanced and not strictly necessary if you simply want to use the cards for divination. However, to fully appreciate the significance of the Tarot, you need to be aware of these issues, even if you do not wish to explore them any further.

In this chapter, we will examine the internal structure of the Tarot pack. We will endeavour to understand why the cards carry the divinatory meanings they do – which should make them easier to remember – and also set the stage for putting our new knowledge into practice not merely for divination, but by introducing a little magic into our daily lives.

Many students of the Tarot find that meditating on the meanings of the cards one by one is an effective way to explore their own psychology and inner urges. Although the intimate details of this inner landscape (or mindscape) are unique to each one of us, there are many significant features that are common to all of us, such as love, hope, fear, greed etc. Once recognised and understood, it is possible to balance and integrate these powerful forces within ourselves.

The two-fold goals of this process are simply to become less prone to falling foul of the trials of everyday life, and to gain greater personal energy or empowerment. Obviously, progress towards either of these goals would enhance anyone's quality of life, so a steady improvement in both will afford the student the very desirable benefit of greatly increased enjoyment of life. Of course, mystical experiences and magical moments may also accompany you on this important voyage of self-discovery.

The veil of symbolism

An ancient oriental proverb succinctly reveals the traditional three stages of mystical experience. Firstly, to every uninitiated person a mountain is simply a mountain, and a stream simply a stream. To the initiated novice, however, a mountain is the embodiment of aspiration, enduring truth, and inner peace (etc.), whilst a stream is the living symbol of the flow of time, life, consciousness and so on. Finally, for the enlightened master, the mountain is once more a mountain, and a stream a stream.

Therefore, to learn the secrets of the Tarot, we should anticipate a journey through a strange and haunting realm of symbolism where nothing is what it seems, and everything offers a secret message. These clues will, so the tradition assures us, fit together perfectly as building blocks that form an invisible temple around us. When the final piece of this spiritual jigsaw is put in place, the entire structure is suddenly revealed in a flash of enlightenment. Here we may achieve the knowledge of and communication with the divine (of which all things are a part) that all mystery schools profess to teach.

In order to free ourselves from the powers of illusion and the misery that it brings, our task is to learn to recognise the significance of visual appearance, pierce the veil of illusion, and discover the truth beyond the symbol. A weighty proposal and not, you might be forgiven for thinking, for the faint-hearted! Just remember this: it is a particular virtue of the Tarot that you can take it one step at a time, one card at a time, and that each one contains an inexhaustible treasury of valuable gifts.

There is also another useful antidote that can prevent us from getting too wound up in impenetrable language and mind-boggling images of mystical experience. Omnipresent deity resides as much in the ridiculous as the sublime. The Fool, usually regarded as the most spiritual card in the pack, is the perfect expression of this vital principle.

The language of symbols

We are all familiar with road signs that present the driver with a concise visual indication of conditions ahead. Many such symbols are equally transparent once you have learned the *Highway Code*, but others need more careful scrutiny.

118

For example, what of the cross that many Christians wear around their necks? At its most basic level, it is simply a stylised representation of a Roman instrument of corporal punishment. But its meaning for the wearer obviously goes far beyond that initial identification. So it is with any religious symbolism and mystical iconography.

The Tarot is one among many, many repositories of knowledge and insight that have been produced in our species' continuous struggle to understand itself in relation to the universe. Most are systematic, many are internally coherent, and all use symbols, ranging from simple, spoken parables, through complex, colourful mandalas, to elaborate ritual performances.

In fact, our brains are extremely sensitive to pattern recognition. The juxtaposition of light and dark areas that form the human face are a primary example, making it possible to recognise a friend at a considerable distance even at night. Furthermore, we are quick to associate memories and emotions with these images.

Our reactions to many of these stimulating images are learned, and can vary wildly according to the changing fashions of the native culture. Road signs and advertising slogans both rely on our innate ability to continually learn new associations. Others are instinctive, unchanging, and are common to all mankind.

Intuitive responses especially can sometimes be triggered by a situation or image that merely reminds us of the original stimuli. For example, feelings of fear may be aroused by something that presents no real danger, such as a horror movie.

The power of the human imagination is at once a tremendous opportunity for exploring and fulfilling our personal potential and a terrible weakness in the species that has often been cynically exploited by masterful political orators and bogus religious leaders. Blindfolded by a fabric of lies woven into a vision of heaven, many nations have been led, meek as lambs, through hell on earth to their own slaughter.

One of the most important uses of the Tarot for meditation is to untie these bonds, by seeing them as the illusions they really are. By studying them and coming to understand their mechanisms, it is possible to sever the links that produce the conditioned reactions, enabling the student to behave in a free and unfettered way.

The psychological keys that can be operated to manipulate people are also, therefore, to be regarded as stepping-stones to personal liberation.

The many and varied icons and religious images which form a focus for an aspirant's attention are characteristically inherently powerful. They all deserve careful consideration and respect, irrespective of their origin, as they are keys to understanding some or other facet of mankind's collective spiritual experience.

Excluding those teachings that are designed merely to tempt and ensnare the unwary into spiritual slavery, the most mature of these systems offer their novices the prospect of receiving an accumulation of wisdom that has been checked, double checked, and is "guaranteed" to guide the faithful throughout their lives.

It is an essential part of the purpose of most legitimate mystery schools to carefully strip away the layers of the blindfolds that have been built up throughout our lives. Another equally vital part is to equip the initiate with the inner strength and psychic balance to withstand the many temptations that he or she will inevitably face when all inhibitions are removed, and true freedom is attained.

Obviously, if you are studying the Tarot on your own, you will not have the support of a school, but the cards can take the place of a tutor. Using them for divination can be particularly helpful. Even a layout as simple as the Quick Answer should provide profound insights to specific problems that you need explaining.

Although some people prefer to study alone, most enjoy a tendency for sharing information and insights. Communal pilgrimage has always been popular and can be very rewarding. This makes the Internet a particularly attractive proposition, especially for students who live in isolated areas where the opportunities of contact with like-minded individuals is a remote possibility.

The Tarot of Mantegna

Despite the popular identification of the Tarot's Major Arcana with the Judaic system of Qabalism, we would do well to consider, albeit briefly, an alternative perspective.

The Renaissance, of which the Tarot as we know it is a product, drew inspiration from many sources. It was, above all, a melting pot of ideas and ideologies.

The learning of the Arabs and Indians figured highly, especially for the arts of medicine, astronomy and mathematics, but the philosophies of the classical cultures of Rome and Greece especially fired the Renaissance imagination.

Indeed, a particularly powerful influence in Renaissance thought was the remarkable cross-fertilisation of ideas that occurred in ancient Egypt under a succession of Greek pharaohs. Among these was a branch of mystical lore that became known among occultists as the Hermetic art.

Hermetic themes lie at the heart of the Tarot (or Tarocchi) of Mantegna. Before we explore these, we should note that the images were not printed as cards (designed for shuffling etc.), but simply as pictures. Furthermore, to be accurate, the artist Mantegna is almost certainly wrongly accredited with their production, for the style is reckoned to more closely resemble that of the Ferrara school.

Another reason why many modern Tarot scholars have tended to overlook this mid-15th century treasure is that there are no fewer than fifty pictures that may be regarded as belonging to the rank of Major Arcana.

The similarities, however, are arguably more significant than the dissimilarities. For example, certain characters depicted in the Mantegna Tarot are directly reproduced in Tarot packs. Many pictorial elements (such as the landscapes) were also incorporated into later cards. This ancestry is particularly evident in the very influential pack by A. E. Waite, the Golden Dawn initiate.

The main point here is that the Mantegna pictures were specifically designed to provide the student with a completely comprehensive learning tool. It is nothing less than a sort of pictorial encyclopaedia of ideas. When "read" with an understanding of symbolism, these pictures afforded the student a thorough foundation in the best system of knowledge that was available at the time.

Whilst it did not attempt to go into details, the importance of the Mantegna lies in its systematic classification of all of human experience into a series of memorable pictures. Without labouring the point unnecessarily, the primary purpose of these pictures was to teach the pupil the existence of the fifty categories of classification.

Once these were understood, all his or her future experience could be assigned to one or other of these categories, and treated according to the known rules and conventions proper to that particular pigeon-hole. Nothing was left to chance: the gamut ranged from the arts and sociology to astronomy.

I think we can afford a brief digression to consider the pictures. After all, they provide a valuable comparison with the convention of the Tarot that we have inherited. The Mantegna consists of five series of ten pictures each:

1. Social Status. This series starts with the Beggar, equating to the unnumbered Tarot card, the Fool, and progresses through the merchant classes to the aristocracy. Pictures include the Emperor (equating with the Tarot card IV, the Emperor), and the Pope, known in the Tarot as the High Priest, card V.

2. The Muses. The nine Muses are joined by Apollo, their patron.

3. Liberal Arts. Here, the seven traditional liberal arts are joined by three other disciplines, of which Poetry bears an image which has been equated with the Star (card XVII).

4. Virtues. Of these, three have been related to conventional Tarot cards, and even bear analogous titles – Temperance (XIV), Strength (XI) and Justice (VII).

5. The Heavens. Half of these have been directly equated with Tarot cards. The Moon occurs under the same name in the Tarot (card XVIII). Venus has been likened to both the Lovers (VI) and the Star (XVII), Mars with the Chariot (VII), the Sun with its namesake (XIX), Jupiter with the World (XX), and Saturn with both Death (XIII) and the Hermit (IX).

Most readers will feel relieved that I do not consider this the place to delve wholeheartedly into the minutiae of Hermetic and Neoplatonic philosophy! Suffice to say, these 50 cards were held to represent every aspect of life, mundane and spiritual, that a civilised person needed in order to live fully and well.

The same claim is regularly made of the 22 cards of the Major Arcana.

The Tarot story

As a structured summary of all knowledge, the modern Major Arcana is certainly not unique or even unrivalled. It is, however, accessible and versatile.

The unnumbered card, the Fool, depicts a traveller. This has been interpreted as a vital clue to reading the rest of these 22 cards. They are, it is suggested, simply telling the story of a journey.

Indeed, this may be the single most important tale ever told. It chronicles life's great adventure through which the pilgrim soul must travel in its quest for ultimate enlightenment and eternal love.

Every schoolchild knows that an adventure story has a beginning, middle and end. The beginning usually sets out with high hopes and determination, the middle sees the hero or heroine confront impossible obstacles, and the end reveals how the goal was finally achieved, often in a completely unexpected manner. The archetypal adventure runs thus: advance, adversity and accomplishment.

Rather than portraying particular instances, Tarot cards portray archetypes. The Death card, for instance, stands for every form of death, and every possible way of dying, so the cards should be able to tell just about any story. Sure enough, when we look for beginning, middle and end, we find that the Fool symbolises the initial urge, Strength depicts apparent mortal combat with a ferocious beast, and the Universe is the ultimate happy ending wherein everything is accomplished and attained.

Again, please note that although I have given Strength as card number XI (which I have used to represent the half-way mark), it would also be worthwhile for you to consider the impact of Justice being put in its place, as in the Golden Dawn arrangement, etc.

All the other Major Arcana cards in-between these key stages of the adventure simply depict the various elements that occur along the way. Simple and sublime!

Every day has a beginning, middle and end. Every week, every hour, every project, every life … The list is endless, and the Tarot is competent to tell the story of each and every one of these episodes in the great adventure of life itself. This is an important key to using Tarot for divination.

Each one of us is currently involved in numerous projects. These range through mental, emotional, spiritual and physical ventures, and include every aspect of our lives, both personal and public.

A Major Arcana card in a divinatory Tarot reading indicates that a certain stage has been reached in one of these mini-adventures. It is for the Tarot reader to identify which particular one.

Although many Tarot spreads are designed to reveal a sequence of events (the Cycle is a prime example), the experienced reader can divine a sequence even when a Major Arcana card appears to stand alone. Simply by following the numerical sequence of the cards, the reader is able to tell which stage of the journey is due to fall next in the querent's life.

However, if the card is reversed, the whole direction of motion through the Major Arcana is reversed. This means that the card next in sequence to a reversed card is the one numerically before it. This is easiest seen in an example. If the High Priestess (card II) is reversed, the querent's next phase will be influenced by the Magician (card I) and not by the Empress (card III).

In like manner, it is possible to tell how far the client may expect to travel before the particular project draws to its natural conclusion. A reversed direction is literally interpreted as a step backwards. The World (card XXI) is the ultimate goal for every project.

In fact, the idea of progression or step-by-step advance is not confined to the Major Arcana, but is also inherent in the Minor cards, as we shall see when we consider numerology later in this chapter. The main lesson to be learnt by adopting a systematic approach to achieving your goals in life is simply that you can take control of what you do, and do what you will.

For many people, the hard part is deciding that they want something badly enough actually to get up and do something about it! The Tarot reminds us that even the longest journey begins with a single first step ...

A Fool's journey

Any student whose interest in a subject extends beyond the acquisition of an examination certificate will, from time to time, question the tutor's judgement. Mostly the tutor will be turn out to be justified, but occasionally the student brilliantly hits a nail on the head. Imagine the look on Eliphas Lévi's face in the instant he first saw the correlation between the 22 Tarot Trumps and the 22 Qabalistic letters!

I have appended a personal exploration of the Tarot Trumps mainly to demonstrate the importance of not becoming hidebound by tradition, but also to act as a spur for you to undertake your own tour through the cards.

This Fool's Journey is also a good example of the many different layers of meaning that the Tarot can sustain. Initially here, the Trumps represent matters so mundane as to be almost banal, but as the story unfolds, the Fool inexorably delves into very profound matters indeed.

I hope you enjoy the journey ...

The Wayfarer (The Fool)
The Fool embodies the impetus to act, and is as inconstant as a fluttering butterfly. He is overwhelmed by the energy to go out and explore the world, not for personal gain, but simply because it is there.

I   Kit (The Magician)
Control over the four elements of nature (fire, water, air and earth) is symbolised by essential items in any wayfarer's kit; fire-lighting equipment, water bottle, knife and money. These correspond to the four suits of the Minor Arcana.

II   Wit (The High Priestess)
This is the inner resource that every traveller needs. It is the only guide through unknown territory. Without it, even the simplest venture is doomed to court disaster.

III   Neighbourhood (The Empress)
The matriarchal influence may be the Fool's actual mother, but in any event represents the well-known and secure environment in which he grew up as a child. Here the Fool takes his first steps out of the life he has always known.

IV   Country (The Emperor)
The Fool traverses new territory. However, he is still in the same kingdom, and all the rules are the same.

V   Culture (The High Priest)
Although he has now travelled beyond his own land, the religious system is the same, so although the laws may have changed, they are based on the same principles.

VI   Humanity (The Lovers)

Here the Fool is beyond even the reach of the religious system in which he was raised. The only similarities between himself and those he meets are ones which are common to all people, everywhere.

VII   Time (The Chariot)

This long journey has not merely been through space but time itself. The changes that will have taken place in his family home are impossible to imagine. It is time to take stock and reflect on the voyage so far. When the world is so full of differences, how can the adventure be other than eternal?

VIII   Truth (Justice)

Having witnessed and shared so many different ways of life, with vastly different codes of living and wildly different beliefs, it becomes unclear as to who is right and who is wrong. What is to be done? Where is truth to be found?

IX   Solitude (The Hermit)

After saturating his wits with experience, solitude is the only recourse – solitude in which to manage his information overload, and reflect on the bewildering totality of existence. This phase of the journey was not envisaged when the adventure began!

X   Change (The Wheel of Fortune)

Confusion seizes the mind in a turmoil of conflicting ideas, and hopes and fears. Who am I? The only direction that offers the prospect of any progress whatsoever is towards the still point at the heart of the whirling chaos.

XI   Confidence (Strength)

Having struggled free of the preconceptions and automatic responses that he had been taught as a child and which subconsciously governed his actions throughout the journey, there is nothing for it but to trust to himself implicitly. Deliberate spontaneity enters his life.

XII   Experimentation (The Hanged Man)

This is the time to descend from the mountaintop a new man. Allowing himself to be himself is a painful metamorphosis, one in which everyone shares as it forces them to revise their relationship with him.

XIII   Liberation (Death)

The experiment works, however, and he can forge a completely new life for himself, freed from the constraints of his past.

XIV   Competence (Temperance)

His whims are indulged and his talents are explored wherever he goes. Success and failure are met with equal resolve simply to continue.

XV   Mastery (The Devil)

Life is full of strength, activity, joy and creativity. His interactions with people are vigorous to the point where he is indomitable and universally regarded as a natural leader.

XVI   Renunciation (The Tower of Destruction)

With the realisation at the pinnacle of material success that he is still mortal (inescapably doomed to perish and lose it all), the sweetness of his victorious lifestyle is made bitter and insufferable.

XVII   Beauty (The Star)

The world of beauty still surrounds him, but it is shrouded in an appalling spiritual darkness. Ceasing to interact with the outside world, he is inwardly withdrawn, as distant and immutable as a glittering star.

XVIII   Understanding (The Moon)

Dreams and nightmares, inspirations of genius and madness, illusions, phantasms and entire mythologies rise before the mind's eye. Although seemingly real as they capture and hold the imagination, they possess no true substance.

XIX   Insight (The Sun)

As he ceases to strive for any further personal ambition and becomes inwardly still, the world around him is perceived and revealed in greater clarity and detail than has ever been possible before.

XX   Awakening (Judgement)

Such is the perspective of his new insight that he himself is included in the vista as an integral element of life's grand pageant.

XXI   The Wise Fool (The World)

His actions are now entirely harmonious with nature. His inexhaustible energy is applied without guile for the benefit of all, and without fear or favour. His immortality is assured in the enduring legacy that his life's work bequeaths to all future generations, of which he is indivisibly a part.

You will note that I have used the ancient arrangement of Trumps rather than the Golden Dawn or other revisions. Perhaps you would care to apply those changes to the storyline, if you can find the time, and see what happens to the plot ...

A Gnostic view

Some Tarot scholars claim to have detected a Gnostic influence in the Major Arcana. This is a debatable point as not only is the evidence somewhat tenuous, but the Tarot, being deliberately universal in compass, is inevitably capable of supporting many hypotheses. The saying "Seek and ye shall find" is as applicable to the Tarot as it is to life itself.

We would do well to consider every possible insight, so for what it is worth, let us briefly enter the extreme world-view of the ancient Gnostics. There were many Gnostic sects with differing beliefs. However, they shared the notion that gnosis ("knowledge") was the key to personal liberation from mortal woe.

The Gnostics were nothing if not heroic in their estimation of the meaning of life. The entirety of creation was not, they reckoned, the manifestation of divine will, but rather the product of an evil entity whose aim was to ensnare and stifle the spark of divinity that dwells in every human soul.

You can imagine the scale of the problem facing the Gnostics who sought to liberate that holy spark from the morass of matter in which it was buried alive!

Again, the Major Arcana is viewed as a story. For the sake of simple syntax I have assumed the protagonist, the Fool, to be male, but the story is equally valid for either sex.

Before somebody hears of Gnosticism they are, naturally, assumed to be ignorant of the plight of their soul. This state of ignorance is symbolised by the Fool.

The Magician represents the adept (or rather the spark of divinity within him or her) who reveals the true nature of the universe to the ignorant, suffering Fool.

The novice then needs to recognise and reject the illusory and fundamentally destructive powers of mundane government (the Empress and Emperor), exoteric religion (the High Priestess and Pope), and carnal desire (the Lovers). Only then can he embark on his own spiritual journey (the Chariot) to seek the gnosis or knowledge of the ultimate truth (Justice).

Having thereby retreated (the Hermit) and escaped from the temptations and snares of the physical world, the aspiring Gnostic turns his attention inwards (the Wheel of Fortune) and begins the process of confronting and mastering himself (Strength). This involves the systematic renunciation of corporal appetites (the Hanged Man), until mind and body are neutralised (Death).

At this time, the soul's divine energy can flow into and animate the physical frame (Temperance), allowing the individual to engage the enemy (the Devil) in combat. At the climax of this battle, the protagonist discovers the gnosis, and liberation from the bonds of materialism is broken forever (the Tower of Destruction).

Rising through the celestial spheres (the Star, Moon and Sun), the soul is entered into the company of the heavenly being (Judgement), and achieves reunion with God (the World).

With the Major Arcana apparently able to accommodate so many diverse ideas, it is not surprising that some people believe that there is no single "true" solution to their meaning. Instead, they consider the importance of the Tarot is that the cards constantly tempt people to explore all the options and even to devise entirely new interpretations. They are, perhaps, simply a conundrum against which we may sharpen our wits, and this alone would answer the needs of the legendary Fez summit.

Numerology
There seem to be just as many different ways of looking at the Tarot as there are people with eyes.

The subjectivity of human experience has always been a problem for philosophers and mystics alike. It was the very attempt to establish a firm, empirical foundation upon which to construct a new way of understanding the universe, one free from bias and misconception, that was the keystone of the Renaissance.

Of all the techniques at their disposal, geometry and its twin, mathematics, offered an unequivocal and unambiguous science upon which to build a rational worldview.

Mathematics was weaned on observations that the moon waxes and wanes in a steady rhythm, and that the motion of the sun follows a regular course. That these cycles could be measured in terms of days whose number did not vary suggested to the primitive mind that numbers had power over nature. Certainly, they are an integral part of the natural world, and their profound influence, as well as that of symmetry, is still not fully comprehended.

Despite the ease with which it calculates the properties of a universe comprised of as many dimensions as you care to suggest, mathematics remains a recondite and secure language for describing the everyday world. Investigating and understanding the world in which we live is a crucial stage in gaining control over our lives. If we know how something works, we can begin to manipulate that process in order to achieve a different result.

Numerology is a branch of occultism that deals with the properties and powers of numbers. Once understood, numbers (more properly, the forces they represent) can be creatively employed to perform magical sums where working through a formula produces a definite result in the objective world.

Perhaps fortunately, only a rudimentary understanding of this vast subject is necessary to appreciate the meanings given to the cards of the Minor Arcana. A little digression is certainly warranted, after all, numerology inspired the meanings these cards have been given.

Numerologists, like most professional consultants, entertain disagreements between themselves over their working methods. For example, one student might approach numerology from the point of view of astrology, another may prefer working within strictly Qabalistic parameters, a third could be versed in classical Greek geometry, etc.

However, they all share a common basis in the fact that everyone has ten digits on their hands. This is the fundamental reason people tend to count in tens, called Base Ten. If we only had eight digits, it would be natural for us to count in Base Eight. Similarly, if we had twelve digits on each of four hands we might just as easily count in Base 48. This is of fundamental importance when we consider mankind's insurgent interest in understanding extraterrestrial life forms, but this is not the place for such an examination. We may content ourselves with observing *vive la différence*.

Within the contemporary Western Tradition, there is broad agreement on the significance of the numerals from one to ten. These are the ideas that have been assumed to reveal the divinatory meanings of the Minor Arcana cards from the Ace (1) to 10.

1. Unity. This, the first number to be produced out of the void of zero, indicates the union of everything in a complete whole. It demonstrates indivisible and imperishable solidity and strength. It can therefore also indicate indomitable force.

2. Separation. Duality ("This" being distinct from "That") is manifested through a wide range of opposites. A typical example of opposites that are indicated by this number are man and woman. Each is a complementary and essential partner to the other, just like positive (giving) and negative (receiving). Being for (supportive/good) or against (destructive/evil) something is yet another aspect of this pervasive idea. Incidentally, there is more than one sort of duality.

3. Creation. This number represents the power to combine things in order to produce not merely new combinations, but something different. The simplest example is that from two parents, a child, unique and self contained, is born as the third member of the family. The number three expresses the axiom that the whole is definitely greater than the sum of its parts, and embodies the idea of fertility. Creativity provides the inspiration to partake in the magical process of life itself. Naturally, it takes many and various forms.

4. Establishment. Consolidation of resources and the safeguarding of assets are tasks shared by success and failure alike. Taking a stance and making a stand puts one firmly on the map, but whether through choice or constraint, such a position can restrict fluidity of response to changing circumstances. There are many forms of power: this number signifies the power to resist change.

5. Action. Whether carefully considered or blindly impulsive, dynamic movement brings decisive change. Whether the cause is large or small, swift and sudden, or slow and inexorable, once set in motion ripples of effect spread far and wide. Incidentally, according to occult tradition, altering anything involves the protagonist in responsibility for its outcome, as does deliberately doing nothing!

6. Harmony. Balance between opposing forces brings rest and a chance for healing. In a state of calm equilibrium, underlying connections between diverse elements become apparent. Being in tune with one's surroundings encourages the spirit of co-operation and opens the doorway to intimate communion between beings.

7. Fortune. With neither apparent reason nor rhyme, destiny lavishes either good luck or misfortune on all. Curious twists of fate, often disguised as bizarre coincidences, have long been seen as divine (or occasionally, diabolic) intervention. However, the uncanny knack of being in the right place at the right time is a benefit that is perpetually enjoyed by the wise fool who has mastered the art of beginner's luck.

Seven is also traditionally hailed as the number of the perfected individual, a reference presumably to the full complement of the seven planets known to ancient astronomers. The investigation of the relationship between mankind and the universe (seen and unseen) is one of the primary functions of the occult sciences, so seven is associated with mysticism and arcane knowledge. Its particular significance is that it is sufficient unto itself, and requires nothing additional.

8. Intelligence. Understanding of our position in the grand scheme of things enables us to formulate both imaginative solutions to life's problems and practical means of preventing those problems from ever arising. These sophisticated rewards are the products of simple mental processes such as carefully turning things over in your mind, and using the mind's eye to look at situations from other people's points of view.

9. Mystery. This number represents our point of contact with the unknown. Just as intuitive flashes of profound insight may alter forever the way we view the world yet the world itself is unchanged, the number nine can be added to any figure (including itself) and yet be resolved back to the original figure. For example, $6 + 9 = 15; 1 + 5 = 6$). The development of wisdom is our natural reaction to experiencing secrets that can be expressed neither through words nor even in silence. Nine is also regarded as the number of love, perhaps because it is the only means of communicating the incommunicable.

10. Independence. This is traditionally regarded as portraying the interplay between the microcosm and the macrocosm, the core and the whole. For instance, it is the number that describes the dynamic relationship between any individual person and the society within which he or she lives. It represents a major achievement, a sort of coming-of-age where it is now possible to be what you are.

The power of four

The number four is particularly prominent in the Tarot: there are four suits, and four court cards in each suit, giving a total of sixteen court cards, a figure that can aptly be expressed mathematically as "four squared".

To students both of the Hermetic arts and of the Qabalah, four is central to their understanding of the world.

To the ancient Greek mind, the entire universe was composed of four elements: fire, air, water and earth. These four sorts of matter could be ranked in order of subtlety, with fire as the most ethereal element, then air, water, and finally solid earth as the grossest element.

The student of the Hermetic mysteries will readily correlate these four fundamental elements with the four Tarot suits. Over the centuries, a great many other associations have also been keyed into this simple system of classification.

fire	*air*	*water*	*earth*
Wands	Swords	Cups	Disks
south	east	west	north
summer	spring	autumn	winter
noon	dawn	dusk	midnight
warm and dry	warm and moist	cold and moist	cold and dry
choleric	sanguine	phlegmatic	melancholic
(excited)	(cheerful)	(calm)	(gloomy)

With the building blocks of the material universe and even the dispositions of the human mind categorised according to the number four, the Minor Arcana suits are well placed to portray all the events in our lives.

There is also, however, the Qabalistic perspective, which opens up a new line of enquiry. According to this tradition, the number four is not merely linked to the elements that make up the material world, but relates to the process that created the universe in the first place.

In this scheme of things, the four phases of creation begin with the divine urge, sheer will power. The second phase deals with the gathering of the raw materials from which the third phase will emanate. Then comes the fashioning or formation of the raw materials into the semblance of the original idea. Finally, this new creation is awarded independence (which may take the form of simply enduring through time or, if appropriate, being given the capacity for reproduction) so that it can continue its existence indefinitely.

In Qabalism, these four phases (also known as the Four Worlds) are each assigned one of the four letters of the name of the Creator – YHVH (Yahweh, Jehovah). At first glance, it may seem strange that both the second and fourth phases are represented by the same letter – H. The reason for this apparent duplication is basically that the V (phase three) is capable of creatively interacting with its environment (the final H) in a way that is analogous to the way that the initial Y moulded the original raw materials (of the first H).

This is a significant theory. As individuals, each one of us has the power to interact with our neighbours and the world we share in the same creative fashion (albeit to proportionate extent) as the creator of the universe. How we use our personal powers is vital not only to ourselves, but also to our society and the entire natural environment.

Perhaps to emphasise the importance of the contribution each and every one of us makes to our world, in the Minor Arcana these four phases of creation are primarily represented by people – the court cards.

Y	H (first)	V	H (final)
impulse	raw materials	creation	new interaction
King	Queen	Prince	Princess
father	mother	child	family

Inevitably perhaps, the Hermetic and Qabalistic traditions have fused, forming what has become known as the Western Magical Tradition, in which Y is equated with the element of fire, H (first) with water, V with air, and H (final) with earth.

It is also worth noting that the ancient Celtic tradition, especially as found in the myths and legends of Ireland, may also have contributed something to the four Tarot suits. Tarot students who entertain even a passing interest in comparative iconography cannot fail to see a similarity of the suits with the Four Treasures of ancient Ireland.

These Treasures include a spear owned and wielded to devastating effect in battle by the hero, and perhaps, Sun god Lug. The beams of the sun penetrating cloud perhaps clarify this image, or again it may have been associated with lightning as both are aspects of fire. Another Treasure was a cauldron which, like a cornucopia, could never be emptied of nourishing food. Like the Holy Grail, tradition also gave it the power to resurrect the dead. Another was an invincible sword owned by the king of the tribe that brought the Treasures to Ireland. Last, but by no means least, was a pillar of stone that had the power to cry out in acknowledgement of the true king of Ireland.

Wands	*Cups*	*Swords*	*Disks*
Spear of	Cauldron of	Sword of	Stone of
Lug	Dagda	Nuada	Kingship

So with the four-fold divisions in the Minor Arcana and the numerology of the numbers from 1 to 10, we see that these cards can depict a detailed set of particular events and situations in our daily lives.

Taken in conjunction with the Major Arcana, which depict the fluctuating forces that are sweeping us through the particular circumstances of our lives, the Tarot is hailed as providing a comprehensive insight into all aspects of existence.

It is no wonder that when we gaze at a card we can see a world of meaning in its deceptively simple picture.

7

Tarot Magic

What is magic? When we are not talking about the stage magician's art of illusion, the classic definition would have to be "physical change achieved by non-physical means".

In common speech, "to do magic" is accomplishing the impossible. In extreme cases, magic is traditionally able to perform outright miracles. Most magicians, though, content themselves with minor works, using magic as part of a package of measures all focused to the fulfilment of a particular project. Often the goal might be within the reach of an exclusively conventional approach, but what enterprise is so assured of success that it could not use a little extra help?

The Tarot promotes our ability to see the past, present and future as being part of an unbroken chain of events. The story of actions and reactions, causes and effects, that appear during a Tarot reading instil the lesson that everything – even inactivity – produces a directly connected result.

It is in an attempt to capitalise on this natural law that the magician undertakes to achieve results through taking certain arcane actions. These are far removed from those that occupy the time and minds of most people, yet there is not only an ancient tradition that supports the use of magic, but a theoretical basis for its operation. Potentially, there is much to be gained by its use.

Incidentally, it is worth noting that the spirit of the so-called Aquarian Age is always keen to debunk mumbo-jumbo and demystify magic. Modern scholars of occultism would be well advised to be very wary of hiding their personal ignorance behind a veil of needless secrecy. The truth will out, as the saying goes. If the next thousand years is anything like the Zodiac Sign it is supposed to reflect, the sham will be swept clean away.

It is, of course, important not to attempt to use magic for selfish ends or to abuse people. An ancient axiom decrees that such energy will eventually rebound and attack its originator. If, for instance, you do not think you could happily admit to a lover that you attempted Tarot magic when you were looking for love, then you probably shouldn't use it for that purpose in the first place.

There is also a traditional and serious caution that must be acknowledged by any who would undertake feats of magic – to experiment is easy and the method is straightforward – but be warned to choose what you wish to accomplish with very great care. It might just come true!

The future in the cards

There is a school of thought that takes the concept of synchronicity, as already considered in relation to divination, one stage further.

If the cards can somehow connect with the world and be positioned in a spread that reflects real events, perhaps it is possible to reverse the connection.

If this simple idea works, it would mean that we should be able to choose specific cards, deliberately lay them out in a carefully prepared sequence, and allow the connection to mould the world to fit the pattern.

The world is obviously a whole lot bigger than a handful of cards. It would not take too much of a stretch of the imagination to suppose that it might be able to influence the cards. But who could soberly imagine that laying out a few picture cards could change the world?

Such doubts as these are recognised as a serious impediment to the practice of magic. Conventional science does not claim to have all the answers to life's mysteries. Even space and time are ultimately unknown quantities whilst mystical or spiritual experiences are still largely unexplored fields. Perhaps we should not be afraid to try and experiment for ourselves.

Any spread is suitable, although beginners might like to use just one card. Experienced magicians may find that the Celtic Cross is probably the most useful of the traditional spreads, especially as it provides you with the opportunity of giving expression to the origins and obstacles that affect the project. For now we will concentrate on simple rather than complex spreads.

Finding the appropriate cards to position in the spread is at once the most difficult and perhaps most enjoyable part of the operation. It cannot be stressed enough that the choice of cards is crucial to the effectiveness of the effort. Do not begrudge any time spent in eliminating unsuitable cards. Checking and double-checking is a sound investment that could pay handsomely in due course.

Perhaps because the Major Arcana often seem more exciting than the Minor cards many beginners tend to try to use them rather too freely. Such a preponderance of Major cards would tend to fill your life with powerful forces that, if not carefully balanced and harmonious, could engender confusion rather than control progress. The 56 cards of the Minor Arcana should not be regarded as weaker than the Major cards. Their focus is merely more mundane and practical, making them perfect for magical operations that have a clearly defined intention.

Figuratively speaking, the Major Arcana are like the winds that might blow a yacht towards a safe harbour, or into difficulties and onto rocks. You need the right one at the right time! They are best used to move one situation towards another situation rather than as an end in themselves. It is, therefore, vitally important to have a clear idea of the conclusion of your project.

One way of ensuring that the energies of the Major Arcana are channelled into your wished-for project is carefully to position a Minor Arcana card along with it. Both should be clearly visible, although the Minor card ought to be in a slightly subordinate position. For example, if the Major is propped up and leaning against a candelabra, the Minor card should be laid in front of it, flat on the surface. Here we have the appropriate force acting directly on the desired form. This is an ideal arrangement for a simple magical operation.

Of course, there is nothing to prevent the magician from using a series of spreads, each representing one phase of an overall project. In this way it is possible to progress step by step towards achieving a long-term ambition. In fact, this sort of forward planning is often a hallmark of forthcoming success.

You may wish to construct a carefully planned ritual to accompany the laying of the cards in the spread. Note that the guidelines for divination, setting the scene, apply here also. To further bolster the ritual environment, you might decide to extrapolate ideas, colours, and even imagery, from the card that embodies your particular final outcome.

If the card that best portrays your optimum result is the Lovers, for example, you should use as many as possible of your mental associations drawn both from the card and from your own related experience. These may include perfumes, flowers, special clothes (or none at all!), feathers (doves, peacocks, etc.), romantic music, and a great many more personal touches. All these will add to the cumulative power of the ritual experience.

The best frame of mind in which to approach the preparation and performance of any ritual is self-consciously to perceive your actions as simply a part of an inevitable process that is already preordained to be successful. At the climax of an ideal ritual, when the cards are placed into their appropriate positions in the spread, the magician will feel a little like a poker player laying down an unbeatable Royal Flush, for the consequences are assured.

Healing

Attempting to ease the suffering of our fellows is one of the most respectable branches of Tarot magic. It is basically an altruistic act, and brings no specific benefit to the magician, but is undertaken selflessly for the sake of another.

There are a range of cards that may be used. The Sun (XIX) is a good general-purpose tonic. The Empress (III) would be particularly helpful in childbirth. Temperance (XIV) is used to aid during a long recuperation. Where the affliction is chronic and without prospect of recovery, the World (XXI) is usually suggested. These are just a few of the many possibilities, and the Minor Arcana is also replete with beneficial influences.

The technique used is essentially the same as for other purposes, as already detailed. Here, however, an additional card is often used, one that represents the person who would benefit from the particular powers of the healing card you have selected. This additional card is termed the Significator, and acts as a sort of lens through which the healing powers are focused onto the patient.

The Significator is chosen from the court cards. The appropriate rank is reasonably simple to choose, according to the following rule:

The Princess is used for girls and young women (those without offspring).

The Prince is used for boys and young men (those without offspring).

The Queen is used for mature women (especially those familiar with the responsibilities of family life) and the elderly.

The King is used for mature men (especially those familiar with the responsibilities of family life) and the elderly.

Which suit best represents the patient is often rather more difficult to decide. Some people who are familiar with the Zodiac will know that each Sign is traditionally associated with one of the four elements. If the Birth Sign of the patient is known, the suit is easily found:

Wands	*Cups*	*Swords*	*Disks*
Aries	Cancer	Gemini	Taurus
Leo	Scorpio	Libra	Virgo
Sagittarius	Pisces	Aquarius	Capricorn

However, many people prefer the personal touch and invoke their own powers of intuition to guide them in choosing the Significator. If you know the patient personally, it may be possible simply to look through your pack and pick the one that reminds you most strongly of them. Otherwise, you might wish to follow further guidelines based, albeit loosely, on the correspondences of the suits with the characteristics of the four elements.

Wands traditionally represent tall, energetic individuals, and are associated with red hair, freckles, and light brown eyes.

Cups traditionally represent short, passive individuals, and are associated with auburn hair, a sallow complexion, and green eyes.

Swords traditionally represent slim, supple individuals, and are associated with fair hair and skin, and blue eyes.

Disks traditionally represent stocky, sturdy individuals, and are associated with black hair, dark skin and dark brown eyes.

If the identification is still not clear enough, for most people are a mixture of these traits, consult the text detailing the divinatory meaning of the court cards. You should find that the information on the personality given there will enable you to choose their suit. If not, simply shuffle your shortlist of possible candidates, and allow the cards to decide for themselves. Pick one at random!

Note: these complex rules on the choosing of the Significator were formulated centuries ago. Modern magicians may prefer simply to use a photograph of the patient, preferably one showing them when they were healthy.

Designing your own Tarot pack

Why, you might ask, have we taken so much trouble in the preceding chapters to understand the origins and significance of the cards? Is it because through gaining an appreciation of the history of the Tarot you gain the confidence to produce your own pack?

Yes! The reward for struggling through the testing mental exercises in the rather difficult chapter on Tarot Mysteries is a practical one. Do not worry ... this part is a whole lot of fun ...

In our consumer society, we are constantly exposed to the powerful inducements that advertisers strive to produce in order to keep us buying more and more items. For many of us, the struggle to obtain enough money to purchase these tempting trifles ruins not only our happiness but also our health. Worse, despite the implicit suggestions of the adverts, even with all the money in the world we cannot physically buy happiness.

Even surrounded by a wealth of belongings, we can still be emotionally impoverished and feel that we somehow simply do not belong. This is because human beings are, by nature, creative. You might feel like royalty when you are in the process of making a purchase, but when you get home how often does that item give lasting satisfaction?

It may seem daunting that there are as many as 78 cards to make, but believe me, once you have developed a taste for the creative process, you will grieve there are so few. Here again is the beauty of the cards, for as we add to our store of experience and understanding, we become better equipped to put our personal wisdom down on paper and can continually redesign, upgrade and improve our cards. They can become as valuable as lifelong friends.

You do not have to be a skilled artist, or even able to draw at all. The art of collage is a very popular medium with DIY Tarot enthusiasts. With the convenience of modern photography, and the quality, quantity and enormous diversity of pictorial images that are readily available (notably from magazines), there is no problem whatsoever in finding material for creating a collage for every single Tarot card.

Another slightly more challenging source of raw materials is the incessant stream of junk mail that we increasingly receive. There is something rather satisfying about putting those free, glossy adverts to good use rather than simply trashing them.

The basic trick of advertising is to capture the target audience's attention, and one of the best ways to do this is with colour and imagery. The pictures on junk mail can often amount to icons. Many also portray a specific mood. These are usually positive (such as happiness, serenity or arousal), but the darker emotions can also be found (such as greed, anger or fright), although you might have to search further afield for these.

Using the advertising world's persuasive images to create your cards at least guarantees that they will contain a wealth of powerful psychological triggers.

It is, of course, important to avoid the use of trademarks and company logos. Although art enjoys significant freedom of expression, the unauthorised use of corporate imagery is specifically legislated against, so it is generally best to avoid any possibility of complications. To prevent any possible copyright implications, it is also sensible to select your material from several different sources.

Even if your ideal image is too large to fit on your chosen card size, the answer is simple: full colour photocopiers will print reductions to your specifications at a very worthwhile price.

You can make the cards as simple or complex as you like. In many cases, the cards themselves will dictate the design elements. Aces, for instance, are essentially single images (with an appropriate background if you fancy), whereas the 10s or a Major card might benefit from a vast array of related images.

Obviously, if you opt to use a great many layers of paper in the collage, you will also find the complete pack becomes pretty bulky. Likewise, the thicker the materials you use for the collage, the thicker each of your cards will become. Remember that you have got to be able to shuffle 78 of them. One solution to this is to mount your cards onto a series of sheets of A4 (or larger) paper, take them to a photocopier and have them copied directly onto thin card, laminated and guillotined back to their original size.

If you plan to adopt this approach right from the outset, it might be worth considering making the cards a convenient size to guillotine, say 7cms x 10cms. Eight of these fit on an A4 sheet, keeping the entire process within the cost of an ordinary pack bought from a shop. Remember also to leave room for a border around the pictures: photocopiers tend not to scan right up to all the edges of the paper, and the guillotine can use a little room to manoeuvre.

The only real rule is to make the cards the same size, and as large or small as you please. This is your chance to create a perfect fit for your hands, so take a little time practising with a few blank cards of different sizes until you find the most comfortable size and shape.

It is a good idea to cover the cards with a clear plastic sheet which is sticky on one side to keep the collage from peeling or getting dirty. This also strengthens the cards, so that even a thin and flimsy base card will be fine.

It is purely a matter of personal choice whether you make the cards as and when you feel inspired, or work methodically through the entire pack in sequence. If you choose the latter, you might consider starting with the Minor cards in the order – Disks, Swords, Cups, Wands (Aces first, culminating in the King) and then work through the Major Arcana. There are advantages and disadvantages to both approaches. Find which seems best for you.

Once you have assembled the materials from which you will create a card, you may wish to put the pieces together within a ritual environment. Many people find this helps them to use their cards later for meditation and astral exploration.

The main point is really to enjoy the creative act. Do not be put off with thoughts that they won't look good enough. Ask yourself, "Good enough by whose standards?" Anyone who knows anything about the Tarot is going to appreciate that it is all about learning. It's not about previous knowledge or polished talent, but stimulating our ability to learn, and discovering new talents. In an infinite universe there is literally no end to what we can learn. You will not be criticised for the look of your cards by anyone who truly understands them. And if they do not understand the Tarot, don't listen to their criticism anyway! The only criticism you will get from a qualified teacher is if you fail to put enough effort into making the cards – and this is only because they know that you'll never really be satisfied with a half-hearted attempt yourself.

You are your best and only judge. These cards are meant for you. They are made by you, for you. If you like what you have made, keep it, cherish it, and use it. If not, put it aside and do it better purely to please yourself. You cannot lose.

The creative process has always been respected as magical. You are, after all, a god in relation to the inert materials that you are using. And you are making a powerful and mystically significant series of icons. These are sufficient to encompass all human experience. You are creating in your own image.

Learn to do this with the cards and you will come to appreciate and, someday perhaps, master the Great Art, that of life itself.

Exploring the astral planes
Every Tarot card is a doorway to a deeper understanding of the force or situation it represents.

Astral projection is one method of exploring these hidden meanings. It is also the best way for understanding the relevance of the cards to your own life.

The technique used in exploring Tarot cards is very different to that which most people probably think of as astral projection. Many have tried, often with limited success, to project their astral bodies, expecting somehow to see their physical body lying beneath them. Exteriorising consciousness from your body while remaining on the physical plane is a particularly difficult feat to accomplish, although the benefits are, correspondingly, tantalisingly immense. With Tarot cards, the rewards are also invaluable. This method is much easier, too.

Dreamland is the best-known area of the astral planes. Most dreams are simply the product of our minds trying to sort out the events of the day, integrating new experiences into patterns of association so that we can remember and learn from them. But some dreams are much more than that, and purposefully convey messages from our subconscious, ideas that either we could not or would not consider without this inner prompting.

We can all use Tarot cards as a means to access these hidden reaches of the human mind. We can seek and find the messages and insights that otherwise lie dormant until a crisis might awaken them into a startling dream. Imagine how much strength and wisdom could already be stored in the treasure house of your own mind. Also consider how useful it would be if you could bring it into play sooner rather than later.

To enter the astral plane it is only necessary to quieten your physical body and ensure that you have a little time when you can be free from disturbance and distraction. You may choose to lie on your bed, or if you are comfortable with yogic asana, either the Lotus or the Savasana are ideal postures.

Place or hold a card so you can see it clearly. Constrain your eyes to remain within the border of the card, and examine all its components, not only figures and shapes but colours as well. Once you have studied it sufficiently to be able to reconstruct the elements in your imagination, you are ready to begin your own journey of discovery.

Close your eyes and relax completely. As you are welcomed into the soft darkness, imagine that you are passing through an open door. In front of you now a gentle flight of steps leads downwards. Feel free to imagine handrails or any other details that might help you to know you are completely safe and secure. As you descend, you count the steps. Step number 21 brings you to the bottom.

Before you is a passageway with a light at the end: it is an opening. Reaching this opening, you will see a vision of verdant nature. The opening is the mouth of a cave, but you are bathed in warm light from the sun in a blue sky strewn with high wisps of shining white cloud.

The meadow at your feet contains many colourful flowers and is full of luxuriant life. There are trees and birds, and a sense of undying joy.

Other aspects of this realm will make themselves apparent as you become better known there. It is sufficient now to note that there is no element of nature that cannot be found here as well as a fair few that terrestrial nature does not encompass.

However, now is not the time to explore this portion of the astral plane, for shimmering as if out of nothing a vision unfurls before your gaze. It is the Tarot card you have been studying. It is the size of a large door and seems somehow three-dimensional. The image clarifies and grows still.

Approaching it, you can see that it appears to be at the living model from which the card was painted. As you step over the threshold of this magical portal and into the image, it comes to life and you are there in the picture. You might notice movement; there may also be sensations on your skin, such as temperature or wind, sound, and even scent.

You are free to engage figures in conversation. Remember that on the astral plane, it is not only people who can speak. Animals can talk. So can trees, other plants and even rocks. Everything can have its own message for you. Furthermore, literally anything you find or are given could have talismanic powers. These might help you on your journey of exploration in the realm of the card, and may also prove invaluable clues for enhancing your whole life.

To begin with, it is best to stay close to the portal. From this side, the portal looks back onto the meadow and shows the mouth of the cave that leads you back to your waking self. As you become more confident in your astral abilities, you will soon discover that you can conjure this portal simply by wishing it to appear, anywhere and at any time, and it will take you home.

Remember to count the steps as you climb back up the gentle slope of the stairs. The 21st step will bring you to the top, where you can settle smoothly back into your physical frame. Concentrate on deep, rhythmic breathing for a short while perhaps. Slowly open your eyes, and the top door opens into conventional reality once more.

It is very important to take the time to record your journey through the card in as much detail as you possibly can. Most people opt to use a brand new notebook for this purpose, especially when working systematically through the pack in a predetermined sequence, although anything will suffice. Some people use a tape recorder (voice activated is often recommended) and relate their adventure as it happens. Having a trusted friend sit quietly and take notes – as did the ancient scribes – as you describe your experiences is also very helpful, especially if you can take it in turns to explore and compare notes afterwards.

Some individuals report the most astonishing journeys right from their first, encountering all manner of mythical creatures and having bizarre phenomena occurring just about every step of the way. However, such people are rare. Many students experience some difficulty in letting themselves get involved in the astral events. For the journey really to work, the figures and landscape that the card portrays must be allowed to speak for themselves. This is the only way they can offer you their particular messages.

It may take time to relax enough in these strange astral surroundings for you to learn the knack of seeing visions, but it is a perfectly natural ability and, as you can decide to awaken at any time, is safer even than dreaming. If at any point you feel that the vision is no longer representing the card and that instead it is taking an unwelcome turn, you can simply use the portal instantly to leave the astral plane behind.

Occasionally, especially when we are under stress or have a particular issue troubling us, it is difficult to concentrate on anything else and we find our minds keep slipping back to ruminate on the nagging problem. This might certainly distract our attention away from any Tarot card we hope to investigate, but sometimes an answer can be found during these astral journeys to solve the problem.

Even if nothing seems to happen at all, record the way you felt at the time. Above all, persevere. The clues you can find should really open up your mind in a way that is almost always far more entertaining than anything you see on TV.

Seriously, a good journey can offer many surprises. The messages given will be of value not just for helping you to understand yourself, but often have a direct bearing on your day-to-day activities. It is not an empty gesture to suggest that these journeys can transform your life. They equip you with the inner resources needed best to proceed through the great adventure that is Life.

More Tarot magic
If you find yourself in any particular need and are able to identify a suitable card that answers that need, you can project into it and seek assistance.

For example, if faced with a difficult situation at work where you must be confident and stand up for yourself in order to have people see a problem from your perspective, why not try the Emperor?

If it seems that the very act of projecting yourself, meeting the Emperor and explaining your case is exactly the same as the problem you are facing in the objective world, then well done! That is exactly right. It's almost like rôle-play in the privacy of your own mind.

The benefit here is that you can ask the Emperor to give you something to help you overcome your mental block. He might offer you some advice. It may be cryptic, but the meaning should make itself clear later. He may give you an amulet or talisman, perhaps even a totem animal or spirit. He could send you on a challenging quest to find a rare wonder for yourself ... or despatch you with a firm denial of any aid!

Whatever he does will be appropriate to your needs. This might not always be immediately apparent. Sometimes only the perspective afforded by retrospect can verify the truth of the matter. Again, it is clearly important to record your experiences, no matter how trivial or even embarrassing they might seem at the time.

Advanced divination technique

Once again, we now find ourselves in the happy position of being able to reap the rewards of past work.

You can use the technique of astral projection during divination both for yourself and even for a client. Literally enter into each card in the spread and quickly seek the message it has to offer.

This is not an easy manoeuvre because you may lack the time thoroughly to relax and immerse yourself in the experience. However, if you have taken the trouble to design and construct your own pack (which may well be based upon the results of astral exploration of other conventional cards), the investment will now repay handsome dividends. The energy you generated in creating your pack will help to carry you directly into the astral plane simply by imagining that the card lying before you is the shimmering portal.

By projecting your mind into and through the card, without necessarily even closing your eyes, you will instantly find yourself in its familiar astral surroundings. Being already on friendly terms with the astral inhabitants, you are able to receive their messages immediately, and can then transmit them fluently to the client. Naturally, such readings are very different in atmosphere and import from those offered by a relative beginner.

There is yet another clear benefit to these astral journeys, of course. Once you have thoroughly explored the realm that lies behind each of these portals, you will be an authority on the interpretation, significance and power of the Tarot. You will be a guardian and torchbearer of the Tarot for today, lighting the way for those who may come tomorrow.

Like any field of human activity, an expert is defined as someone who knows more and more about less and less. Inevitably, as exploration of a subject continues and discoveries are made, new words are coined to describe previously unrecognised objects or activities.

There follows a short list of words (jargon really) that are either used exclusively by Tarot students, or which have special meanings when used in relation to this study.

Cartomancy. This archaic word simply means "divination by cards". It can equally well be applied to the interpretation of ordinary playing cards as Tarot cards.

Court cards. These 16 cards are part of the Minor Arcana, four being contained within each suit. They are pictured as courtly figures of ascending rank, frequently Princess, Prince, Queen, King. The court cards are often held to represent actual people.

Major Arcana. One of the two parts of the Tarot pack. These 22 cards are numbered from 1 to 21, plus an un-numbered card (sometimes allocated the number 0). These cards have always been fully and freely illustrated with human and animal figures as well as with scenes. They are held to represent the forces that act upon humanity. Successfully dealing with these forces will lead the individual to spiritual attainment.

Minor Arcana. One of the two parts of the Tarot pack, these 56 cards are sub-divided into four suits, usually called Wands, Swords, Cups and Disks. With the possible exception of the court cards, the Minor Arcana are held to represent the situations in which humanity encounters and deals with the forces of the Major Arcana. Traditionally, the cards numbered from 1 (the Ace) through to 10 in each of the four suits were depicted without elaborate illustrations, showing instead, merely pips.

Pips. Small pictures representing the names of the suits of the Minor Arcana. Depending upon the number of the card, the design would show between 1 and 10 pips of the appropriate suit. Pips (usually only one) are also incorporated into the designs of the court cards.

Playing cards. A pack of 52 cards consisting of four suits, often with the Joker, an additional, unsuited card. The suits of playing cards are similar to but not the same as Tarot suits, and are usually Clubs, Diamonds, Hearts and Spades. Here, the court cards lack the lowest rank (the Princess) of Tarot suits. The Tarot rank of Prince is usually portrayed as a Knave or Jack.

Querent. This name is given to the person asking the question for which the Tarot is consulted. This can be (and frequently is) the same individual who is reading the cards.

Reading. A consultation during which the cards are dealt in a spread, and their significance interpreted according to the rules of cartomancy.

Reversed. The name given to cards dealt in a spread that, when turned face upwards, have their normal appearance (inverted with their pictures top to bottom). Reversed meanings may specifically apply to these cards.

Shuffle. This action of disarranging the order of cards in the pack has a slightly augmented meaning to that commonly used with ordinary playing cards. Firstly, not only can the cards be shuffled according to their sequence, but they may be rotated to provide reversed meanings. Furthermore, the intention in a Tarot reading is not merely to disassociate cards with their neighbours, but to allow them to arrange themselves in such a way as to answer the querent's question.

Spread. The pattern into which the cards are dealt for a reading. As a rule, the position occupied by each card has a unique meaning that is taken into consideration along with the interpretation of the card itself.

Suits. These are the four sets that contain all the cards of the Minor Arcana. Usually the suits are named, and illustrated, with pictures of Wands, Swords, Cups and Disks. Each suit contains a sequence of cards numbered from 1 (or Ace) to 10, plus four court cards.

Tarot cards. A pack of usually 78 cards, comprising both the Major and Minor Arcana.

Trump. Any card of the Major Arcana.

Index